Hope

for Tomorrow

My Story for *His* Glory

CATHERINE ALBEANESE

Fair Havens
PUBLISHING

To my beautiful daughter, who has taught me more about living and the beauty that life can be. You, my precious one, have blessed me, thrilled me, and comforted me on this journey. Thank you for always trusting when I've heard from God, listening, and encouraging me along the way. You are truly a precious and beautiful cherished gift from Him. I couldn't have made it without you.

To Mary, even though you are now reaping all your rewards in heaven, I want to thank you for pouring your life, knowledge, and wisdom into me. I would have never come to know the Lord the way I do had it not been for you. I will always remember your patience and kindness. When you entered the gates of heaven, I know you heard, "Well done, my good and faithful servant."

IS THIS MESSAGE FOR YOU?

THE STORY YOU ARE ABOUT TO READ isn't easy to tell. It's about a life full of pain and problems but also of hope, freedom, and deliverance. Many will wonder why anyone would reveal such dark, intimate details, and many may ask why one would uncover such things.

This story isn't for the people whose lives are happy and problem-free. This story is for the lost, hopeless, and depressed who think life will never get any better and who function from crisis to crisis. It is my hope that reading my story will help you find what I found and that you will finally be able to walk in freedom and the destiny God has planned for you.

PREFACE

I REMEMBER TELLING THE LORD when I first got saved that if the second half of my life would be anything like the first part of my life, to please take me home. I just didn't feel like I could go on living. Every day was a struggle just to exist. That was when I was twenty-nine years old. It wasn't until I was thirty-nine, almost forty, before I would start to have a ray of hope.

In May of 1990, I left New Orleans with my beautiful nine-year-old daughter and moved to Georgia. Oh my. It seems like it was yesterday. I was terrified! My daughter was dependent on me, and I knew that whatever decisions I made would affect her for the rest of her life. The stress was incredible, but living in New Orleans under the conditions we lived in drove me to make the decision to leave.

Arriving in Georgia was the beginning of miracle after miracle. If you never walk through the valley, you never get to experience the awesomeness, the power, and the miracles of God. He was the one who guided me, directed me, led me, and showed me the way. He opened doors and made the crooked path straight. The blessings He poured on us were incredible, and I am still humbled at the thought of them. I learned that *nothing* is impossible for Him.

Yet, I still wonder at times why I was born into the family I was born into and why I had to experience the things I endured. I know this: even though it was rough, I would never have come to know the Lord like I do if I had not gone through those things.

The trials of life form you and mold you into the person you become. God uses everything that comes into your life to mold, shape, and make you into the person He created you to be. Nothing is wasted with the Lord. Every tear you cry, every fear you feel, every crisis you go through, and every person who comes across your path, He uses. Before He formed you, He knew you. He knit you in your mother's womb, and your substance was always before Him.

Of course, until we come to know the Lord, we have absolutely no idea why we are here and if there's a plan and purpose for our life. We aimlessly go through life, living from circumstance to circumstance, and we often let those circumstances define who we are.

Once you come to know the Lord and learn that you can trust Him, you see that He can turn all things for your good and that the "real you" is very different from the circumstances that formed you. You quickly learn that you are stronger than you thought, and you can do all things through Christ who strengthens you.

Of course, when you are going through those trials, you don't see anything but the dark clouds and tempest you are in. It isn't until after the storm passes that you look back and see and learn from what you went through, and then you are amazed that you survived.

PART ONE

A Child of Sorrow

Chapter
ONE

I WAS BORN INTO an affluent family. My dad was a multimillionaire who had nine different businesses. I lived with my parents, paternal grandparents, and brother, who was seven years older than me.

I was born with an enlarged thymus, a lymphatic organ located behind the breastbone in the chest. As a result, I was watched twenty-four hours a day so I wouldn't choke to death. When I was three days old, doctors began radiation treatments on me to shrink my thymus.

My mother told me I was a difficult child from the beginning. She had to keep me quiet so that I wouldn't choke. If she took me out around many people and I had a lot of stimulation, I would stay up all night crying.

My mother said things that would stick with me for years to come. She told me that I could never be loved enough. She said they wouldn't take a million dollars for me, but they wouldn't take a million to have another one like me. I could never figure out why I felt so unloved until years later. I always felt like there was a hole in me. I never felt wanted or cherished.

The messages you receive, even as an infant, can
end up turning into strongholds later in your life.

In spite of these strongholds taking shape inside of me, I was pretty spoiled. We traveled a lot, and I had big, expensive birthday parties, lots of clothes, and toys. I was even given my first scuba diving tank when I was nine years old, and at age ten, I was diving under the oil rigs out in the Gulf of Mexico with my dad.

Life was good until fourth grade. From that point on and into young adulthood, my life was in constant turmoil. My parents discovered my private school was nine months behind the curriculum of the Catholic school near us. My mother decided that was not acceptable, as everything and everyone in her family was smart and perfect. So, in the middle of fourth grade, I was moved and put in the advanced class since I had been making straight A's.

I struggled in fourth grade in more ways than one. I remember trying to learn my multiplication tables one night. My mother couldn't understand why I was having problems. I was surrounded by nuns who were—let's just say not the heavenly charitable people they professed to be. My mother and I began to have some conflicts regarding the Catholic religion. I witnessed the behavior of the nuns and the priests who portrayed a God who was nothing like the God I wanted to know.

In grammar school, we were required to go to confession every Tuesday. I would get so nervous that I would make up sins to tell the priest because I didn't know what else to do. The priest would always tell me to say a rosary for penance, but I didn't do this. The rosaries were redundant and made no sense to me. I never understood the teachings of the Catholic Church, and what I was going through didn't make it any easier to accept. Don't get me wrong; there are many wonderful Catholics who really love the Lord. That's just not the type of faith that was shown to me.

The little I knew about God was that He was patient, loving, and kind— not critical, judgmental, and harsh. He certainly would never deliberately humiliate you in front of people like these people who were supposed to represent Him did. During recess, I would go into the church and talk to God. I remember telling Him I knew He was there, but I felt like He was so far away. I didn't feel like I could reach Him. He seemed so distant, yet I wanted to be closer to Him. I would sit there and tell Him how miserable I was, and I would feel some semblance of peace until the bell rang and I went back into the strict rules of the school. That peace helped sustain me for what was ahead.

I had many substitute teachers because my regular teacher was hospitalized multiple times for mental health problems. I barely passed into the fifth grade. Then in sixth grade, my whole life changed. I was still struggling in school, trying to learn a new math called sets, when my mother went into the hospital with a ruptured appendix. My dad had been out of town, and she had been very ill but refused to go to the doctor. She waited for him to come home and sleep for eight hours before telling him how sick she was. He then rushed her to the hospital, where she had emergency surgery. We were told she might not live due to the infection she was fighting. She remained in the hospital for weeks before she could come home.

A few days after my mom went to the hospital, I fell asleep in my dad's bed while watching television. The television was in my parents' bedroom, not in the living room where most families kept their televisions. Every night, I would lie in bed with my parents and watch TV until it was time for me to go to bed. The only difference this time was that my mom wasn't there when I fell asleep. I was awakened in the middle of the night by my dad touching me inappropriately. I didn't understand what was happening. I was so ashamed and embarrassed and didn't know what to think. The next day, he told me that I couldn't say anything to anyone because I would destroy the family if I did. I was eleven years old and felt like the weight of the world was on me.

This brought a feeling of worthlessness and shame that would take years to overcome. The world became jaded, and I felt like people were looking at me, knowing what had happened to me. I was afraid to say anything because I didn't want to destroy my family and possibly be taken away from them.

When this happens to a child, the perpetrator seems to disregard the horrific damage it causes. Children who are abused may constantly wonder what is wrong with them and what they did to cause that to happen to them. They can develop low self-esteem along with a poor body image and feelings of worthlessness. This ends up affecting every relationship they have, whether with men or women. They are suspicious of everyone they meet and never let anyone get too close. Basically, they have trust issues.

Then, as time passes, they may feel out of control. Since they feel like they have lost all control, anger and rage begin to develop, and they stuff all those thoughts. But one day, the feelings come out. They manifest anytime they start to feel out of control, and God help the person who is on the receiving end of their fury. Of course, I didn't know any of this for a very long time. I didn't want to be that way, but life was unstable all around me.

My mother survived and came home. I was relieved she was back. Maybe then I wouldn't have to go through any more shame and humiliation. That year was very difficult because I mentally checked out. I couldn't concentrate at school. I started failing most of my classes, going from B's to D's and F's. When I brought my report cards home, my mom would yell, scream, slam cabinet doors, and throw things. My dad would come home in the evening after I had been crying all afternoon and say, "You will do better next time, right?"

CHAPTER ONE

Now I know why he never yelled. He knew he was the reason I was having so much trouble in school. I began to feel worthless and stupid and couldn't understand what was happening to me. My whole family would hear Mom's yelling, and everyone would stay in their rooms for a few days until the storm was over. The kids at school knew I was failing and would give me pathetic looks that seemed to say, "You poor thing, you're failing because you are stupid." It was so humiliating to watch my friends go on to the next grade, knowing I would not be going with them.

My failure put a bigger wedge between my mother and me. My cousins didn't have any problems in school yet. I was the black sheep of the family. My parents had me tested at another school, and I failed the entrance exam. I was so confused and continued to live "out in space" somewhere. When situations got tense, I would "check out." I couldn't concentrate or focus on anything.

Not long after these problems at home and at school began to develop, my grandfather started fondling me and kissing me inappropriately. I had no place to run or hide. This abuse went on for about three more years. I couldn't understand how three other adults were living in the house, yet no one knew what was happening to me, or so I thought. I learned how to protect myself as best I could by making sure I wasn't alone with my father or grandfather. Everything on the outside appeared to be as normal as possible, but on the inside, I wanted to die.

I repeated the sixth grade and made it into seventh, where I had a teacher who basically taught us to lie. She would leave the room to go to the office, and when she came back, she would ask who talked while she was gone. We would raise our hands, and she would methodically take down our names and take points off our conduct grades for the week. We started every week with one hundred points. Then, throughout the week, she would take points off for talking, forgetting your beanie, not having your tie, or not having your shoes polished. At the end of the week, anyone with a ninety-four or below in conduct would receive "punish work" for the weekend. We were assigned twenty-five spelling words to be written fifty times each, and their definitions were to be written twenty-five times each. I had punish work every weekend.

On Monday, if you didn't do it or if it was incomplete, she doubled the work. Many of the kids began lying when she would ask who talked. I was probably one of them. One day, I decided I had had enough of punish work, so I decided I wouldn't do it ever again. That weekend, I lied and told my parents I didn't have punish work. Monday came, and the first thing we were asked to do was pull out our punish work. When the teacher got to me, I told her I didn't have it. She announced it was doubled. I replied that I was not ever doing punish work again. Her face turned beet red.

"You will stay in at recess today to start," she said.

"All right," I replied.

Recess came, and I just sat there. The teacher said, "You better get started."

I quietly replied, "I told you I'm never doing punish work again."

"Well, you will sleep here tonight if you don't do it," she said.

I told her I was prepared to sleep on the floor if I had to because I would not do any punish work. School let out that day at two thirty in the afternoon. I usually walked home, but that day, I was still sitting at my desk at four o'clock. My mother came looking for me and discovered I was sitting at my desk. She motioned for me to go to the car. My teacher was at her desk and told my mom I had not done my punish work and that I was refusing to do it. I chimed in and told her I was never doing punish work again. My mom told me to go to the car.

I walked out of class and did as I was told. When my mom got to the car, I told her I couldn't do any more punish work, and if she and Dad wanted to punish me at home, that was okay with me. I had decided I would take up for myself even if no one else would. That's when she told me not to worry, as I was not ever going to do punish work again, and for me not to say anything to the other kids.

Eighth grade was another story. As usual, I was having problems with math and was failing. I had to go to summer school so I could pass. At the end of the year, my friends and I were to graduate before going on to high school. Of course, because I was failing math, I was told I wouldn't be allowed to participate in the graduation ceremonies. Still, the nuns told my mother to send me to graduation practice so that no one would know that I would not be graduating with my class. When the day came to practice for the graduation ceremonies, I was sent to school even though I asked not to go.

The gym was filled with all four eighth grade classes—around one hundred and twenty kids. One of the nuns called two other students and me up to the podium and announced that we were excused and could go home since we would not be graduating. We didn't even participate in the practice. We were so embarrassed, humiliated, ashamed, and angered at what they did to us. I was never so glad to leave a place in my life.

I left school but didn't walk home. Instead, I went to the levee, where I often went when I wanted to be alone. My mother would always tell me not to go there because the hobos would get me. I hoped they would, especially that day. It was dark before I got home. When I told my mother what had happened, she defended the nuns because, after all, they would surely never do anything like that. This only reinforced the beliefs I was forming on my own, and they were not necessarily Godly beliefs.

When it was time for high school, my dad sent me to a private Christian school. He had spoken to the principal and explained to him that our family traveled. My dad made arrangements with the principal for times I would not be in school and then made large contributions to the school so there would be no problems with my being absent. I was given all my work and did it when we traveled. I took any tests that I missed when I got back. High school was so much easier for me. Besides, my dad knew I was fed up with

Catholic school, and my mom and I were still having arguments over the Catholic religion.

Because of my conflict with my mother, I began to see how she wanted everything to be perfect in her world. If she didn't like something, she would rewrite it in her mind. Her reality was quite different from the real world.

During high school, I took a Bible course. Being Catholic, we—my mother's generation, mostly—had been forbidden to read the Bible. This carried forward into my generation as well. We were told that the priests were the only ones who could interpret the Bible correctly. I began to read scriptures that said we were to call no one father, as there is only one Father, and He is in heaven. I also read scriptures that said not to say repetitious prayers and explained how we were to pray. I began to question the teachings of the Catholic Church.

My mother was unhappy with me. She said we were not to question but just believe. My dad, on the other hand, allowed me to question things and would listen to my opinions. He was the only one who seemed to value what I thought or said. I loved the Bible stories and felt peace when reading and listening to them. Still, I look back and realize I wasn't mentally present in most situations. That is how I coped.

Chapter
TWO

I CAN RECALL when I was five or six years old and my father took me to a woman's house. I was there with her kids and just the two of them, and I remember her wearing a black negligee and him chasing her around the house.

By the time I was eighteen, my dad had begun to lose everything. He had a business partner, and together they owned a motel and marina in South Padre Island, Texas. I spent many summers there, walking on the beach alone. I would stay gone for hours, either walking or, if I had a board with me, surfing. I didn't have any friends there, so I fished, swam, and surfed by myself. My dad's partner wanted out of the business, so my father told him he would buy him out. One year, a hurricane hit, causing one of the businesses to shut down for nine months. My dad didn't plan on the business being closed for so long, and one by one, all his companies went down like a row of dominos.

God will often allow trials to come into our
lives to get our attention and open our eyes
so we can take an inventory of our life.

Looking back on that time, I believe God was trying to get his attention. My father's life was getting out of control. He loved women and was an entrepreneur who loved the art of the game.

My dad was in Chicago, trying to get financing, when I came home from school one day and found that all the furniture in our house was gone. Our beds, clothes, a dining room table, and some dishes were the only things left. My grandparents were at the dining room table, crying. I remember telling them we had to get some boxes to put everything away. The dishes were on the floor, and our clothes were on our beds. I wasn't upset over the loss of everything, as material things didn't mean anything to me at that point. I was too busy trying to survive the emotional chaos in the house—the yelling, rages, and fighting among my parents and grandparents.

During this time, I found out my dad was having affairs with different women. That's when I realized what the deal was with the woman in the black nightgown I had seen him chasing years earlier. My mother would confront him and go into rages. Often, she would take her anger and frustration out on me. Neither of my parents realized I knew what was going on. There was no way I would talk to my mother about his indiscretions. It was years later before my dad understood that I knew what was going on. So many secrets were kept in that house.

My brother had already moved out of the house when all of this was happening. He married when I was thirteen years old. I cried the entire day of his wedding. My parents had to take me home because I couldn't stop crying. I knew his wife didn't really love him because I had overheard her say words to that effect. She was marrying him to get out of her house. Was anyone happy? Was this the way life was for everyone? Little did I know that the tears I cried that day would be significant in later years and were a fore-shadowing of what was to come.

When we lost the house, my father came home and held a family meeting. He had managed to come out of everything with about $12,000. He began to divide up the money and had already purchased a house for my grandparents. I remember my grandfather asking him if he was finished with his meeting. My dad told him yes, that was all he had. My grandfather told him he wasn't satisfied; he wanted all the money and the house. A fight began, yet I could see the hurt and pain in my dad's eyes. I couldn't believe money was more important to my grandparents than my dad was.

As we prepared to move out of the house, the tensions grew. There was no furniture, and we were moving to an apartment. As we were packing household items, my grandmother began fighting with me over the dishes. I didn't know my dad was in the house when I threw a plate on the floor and told her to take all of it.

"We don't want any of this!" I yelled.

My dad came in and began yelling, too. I left and went to the levee to get away from all of them.

Not long after we moved into an apartment, we found out my mother was pregnant. What a shock! I was nineteen years old and tried to look at it with some excitement. Maybe this would be a ray of light that would bring some happiness. That was short-lived. When she was four months along, she lost the baby. I had gone out with some friends when I got a funny feeling and told them I had to go home. When I got there, my mother was in the bathroom having a miscarriage. The baby was still attached to her. I grabbed a towel and gently picked it up so my mom could lie down, as she had been sitting on the toilet when this happened. It was a little girl with tiny little hands and feet. I felt so bad for my parents. I called my dad, and he came, and we took Mom and the baby to the hospital.

During this time, I landed a job at a phone company as a directory assistance operator. I saved some money and was able to buy us a bedroom set. I took the dresser and gave the large chest to my parents. We were finally able to move our clothes out of boxes and into some furniture. I was glad I could help but didn't realize the effect it would have on my dad. He was happy for us but dejected because he couldn't provide it. He wanted me to go back to college. I had gone to school in West Palm Beach, Florida, for one semester but had to come home due to a lack of finances.

I did take some courses at the University of New Orleans, but with my academic history, I was sure I would be a failure. I dreamed of being a doctor but knew I wouldn't make it. Besides, my dad would never allow me to be in medicine. He felt that it was a demeaning profession. He was Italian and had some pretty old-fashioned ways. He didn't mind me working but would never allow me to deal with people's medical problems. I was floundering, trying to figure out the purpose of my life. I had no direction.

After we lost everything, my father began working with my brother, who had his own business making some type of radios for boats. I could tell my dad wasn't happy. He was used to wheeling, dealing, and making things happen in his own world. Somehow, he convinced my brother and mother that it would be good for all of us to go on a trip to the Virgin Islands. We had been to the Caribbean many times before. It was always my dad, mom, and me, and my dad and I would scuba dive or snorkel all day long. One year, we spent an entire summer on a houseboat, going from island to island diving and meeting all kinds of interesting people. This was when my dad had money. Now he was broke. My mom and brother could see how miserable he was, so they agreed to go. I'm sure they thought this would bring him some happiness.

The trip was in July before I turned twenty-one in August. We rented a houseboat, and for two weeks, we went from island to island, spearfishing, catching lobster, and cooking on the boat every night. It was so beautiful: crystal clear blue water during the day and millions and millions of stars at night. At the end of the two weeks, we returned to New Orleans and life as usual. Or so I thought.

Not long after we returned, my brother came over one morning to talk to my mother. I went to work and didn't know where my dad was. When I got home, my mother and brother were still sitting at the kitchen table. I could see they had both been crying for what must have been a very long time. When I asked them what was wrong, they both stared at me for the longest time before they spoke.

Finally, my brother said, "I walked in on my wife and Dad having sex in my bed."

His wife, the woman I had cried over for an entire day when she married my brother. A flood of emotions hit me: anger, rage, and feelings of murder, to name a few. How could this have happened?

I was told it had started on that houseboat out in the middle of the Caribbean. It wasn't a big boat. I wanted details. I was told it began when the two of them had been left alone on top of the boat at night, looking at the stars in the sky. Sick to my stomach, I went up to my room and closed the door. I didn't want to see any of them. The word shock doesn't describe what I felt.

The next three weeks were unbearable, surreal, and unbelievable. In the midst of such insanity, it's funny how God comes to your mind. The big family Catholic Bible that no one read was in a box in the closet. I got it out and started flipping through it. My mother asked me what I was doing.

"There must be something somewhere in here that can tell us that what he and she are doing is wrong," I said. I couldn't find it, though, and ended up laying it aside, never to open it again.

Every day, some horrific crisis would happen. At one point, I called the house for my brother, and his wife answered the phone. We got into a huge fight. I told her I was on my way over there to wipe the street up with her. Before anyone knew it, I was in the car and had backed out into the road when the vehicle stalled. I couldn't get it to start, and my mother came running out, begging me to get out of the car and come back inside. Now when I look back, I can see that it was the hand of God that saved me from myself that day. I was in a blinding rage and would have killed her.

My sister-in-law told my dad what I had done and said to her. He came home in a rage. From my room, I could hear him screaming, "I'm going to kill her first, then I'm going to kill you!" I found the phone, called the police, grabbed a gun, and hid in my closet. I was terrified. I heard screaming and crashing noises, then total silence.

I stayed in that closet with the gun cocked, waiting for the door to open. I did not doubt that I would shoot whoever opened that door. No one came. Finally, I heard a small, pitiful voice say, "He's gone. You can come out now."

I went downstairs and saw the carnage that had taken place. We had solid oak captain's chairs, and one of them was stuck in the wall above the dining room table. The table was cracked down the middle, and my mother was sitting in another chair. The stove had been kicked in, and glass was everywhere.

Then, there was a knock at the door. It was the police. I invited the officers in and tried to explain to them that the man who had done this was my dad but that something was terribly wrong because the man I had known as my father would never have been so violent. He would not have done anything like what I had seen and heard. I asked them to stay long enough for us to pack a bag so we could leave. My mother said she wasn't leaving her home. I told her we were because I knew he would be back.

CHAPTER TWO

In 1971, police didn't want to get involved in family arguments. They wanted to leave. I begged them to give me five minutes, and then they could go. I packed as fast as I could. The police left, and we got into my car. As I started down the street, I looked in the rearview mirror and saw my father headed toward us. I drove as fast as possible to the interstate, and he followed us. I was going ninety-five to one hundred miles per hour, weaving in and out of traffic. I finally exited the interstate, pulled into the back of a fast-food restaurant, and sat there. We had lost him.

After sitting there for quite some time, we decided to drive to my dad's sister's house, where we stayed for four or five days. During that time, my mom was talking to my dad. He had agreed not to come home and said that we could go home, and he wouldn't bother us there. By this time, my aunt and her family knew all the ugly details about what was happening. I told my mom and my aunt that I thought my father was mentally ill and that he had had a nervous breakdown. I wanted to have him committed, but the family felt he would talk his way out of being hospitalized. They would have kept him for seventy-two hours and then probably would have released him.

He was staying in a hotel, but I didn't know which one. I just knew what part of town he was in. We went back home, but life certainly wasn't normal. But then again, it had never, ever been normal.

I was twenty years old and on edge all the time, never knowing what would happen. My brother was still living at his house with his wife and three small children. How he continued to live there, I don't know. Not long after returning home, I went to my brother's house to see him. When I walked in, my sister-in-law was sitting at the kitchen table with my dad. He looked at me and said, "Why won't you give me some time with her? I deserve that much."

I lost it. I remember exploding and telling my dad, "I never want to see you again! I'm sorry I have ever listened to you all these years! I never want to see you, and if I ever have children, I never want them ever to see you or know who you are."

I walked out and left. My brother was in his garage, working on one of his boats. I felt like I was living in the twilight zone. I went home and told my mother what had happened. Everything about the rest of that night is a blur. I don't remember anything except how I was feeling. Was anyone sane? How I wanted to just disappear.

Chapter
THREE

THE NEXT MORNING around eight o'clock, my cousin knocked on the door. We had not told her anything, so I was shocked to see her. She walked in and handed me my dad's wallet and a letter. She said he had driven to her house, knocked on the door, and given her his wallet and an envelope, which had a nine-page legal-sized letter in it. My mother and I sat down with my cousin and began to read the letter. Most of it made no sense. It was just a lot of rambling. The only part I remember was that he told my mother and brother that I was the light, that I had the light, and that they should listen to me. We sat there all day, waiting and trying to figure out what was going on.

My mom had even started to cook dinner when there was another knock at the door. It was our family doctor. I was so surprised to see him, and I remember asking him why he was there. He came in and told us there had been an automobile accident. My dad had lost control of his car and driven off the causeway into the lake.

"I'm so sorry," he said, "but he's not coming home."

My mother began to cry. My uncle, who had been standing outside until the doctor gave us the news, came into the house. Immediately, I got up from the table and asked if anyone wanted coffee. I thought, "This is some kind of sick joke they are playing," and I felt it couldn't be true. I walked into the living room and turned on the television. The news came on, and I saw a clip of the police pulling my dad's body out of the lake and putting him on a boat.

The mind is an incredible thing. Even though I saw that scene with my own two eyes, I still didn't believe it. My uncle called my brother and asked him to come over but did not tell him why. In the meantime, the doctor could see I was going into shock. He gave my mother a shot to help calm her down and was preparing to give me a shot as well. I told him I didn't need it. I was busy making coffee. He started to walk over to me with the medicine, and I began to run. I knew if he stuck me with that needle, it would be real, and I didn't want any of what they were saying to be real. He and my uncle grabbed me and tackled me to the ground. I screamed and tried to fight them off, but they were too strong for me.

Whatever was in that shot, it didn't take long to take effect. I felt numb, very strange. I had no feelings at all. My brother arrived, and they told him what had happened, then gave him a shot. He didn't want it, but I told him to take it because it would help him. All kinds of people began showing up at the house. I couldn't cry or sleep. I was up all night. In those days, the TV went off at midnight. I just walked around the apartment or sat on the bed, looking at the ceiling for the rest of the night. My mother stayed in her room in bed. I remember calling some of my friends and telling them my dad had died. I never told any of them the gory details. Over the years, I had learned never to let anyone in on the truth of what was going on in the family. I was good at hiding things.

My brother went to the coroner's office to identify the body. He wouldn't let me go. Later, he went to the funeral home and made the arrangements. He came home and said he had chosen a hermetically sealed coffin for him. The cost was astronomical. We didn't have any money. My dad had driven the only car my mom had into the lake. I told my brother to go back and get the cheapest coffin they had because Dad wasn't there anyway, and we would be left to deal with the bills. It's sad to think how people can take advantage of you when you are going through such a crisis.

On the day of the viewing, my mother, brother, and I went in to see him alone. We walked in, and my mother said, "That's not my husband," and walked out. I told my brother to close the coffin because Dad looked like a monster. It was horrific. I walked out and went to be with my mother. I had told my brother not to bring my sister-in-law to any of the services, and he respected my wishes. I sat upstairs with my mother, and I could hear my grandparents screaming because the coffin was closed. My brother came up, and I told him to open it if that would shut them up. My mother did not attend the funeral. She stayed home instead.

I still hadn't cried. I just couldn't. I could overhear some of my family members giving opinions to each other as to why I wasn't crying. I felt like I was on the outside of myself, watching a movie, and none of it was real.

> It amazes me how people judge you even when they have absolutely no idea what you are going through or what you have been through.

I remember hearing, "She never loved him. If she did, she would be crying." "She hasn't shed one tear." "Where's her mother?" "Why isn't she here to bury her husband?" People can be so cruel with such awful judgments and accusations. Why did I have to live through this? Everyone else's life seemed to be so normal. I never knew what normal was. I did know, however, that my family was very different.

Time passed—just how many days, I don't remember—and I got a call from my sister-in-law. We had not spoken since the day before my dad committed suicide. She was frantic and said she had gotten a call from my brother telling her to kiss the kids goodbye for him and tell them he loved them. Then he hung up. She didn't know where he was or what he was planning to do. I hung up with her and waited. Surely, he would call Mom to give her the same message. The phone rang, and I grabbed it. It was him, and he started to talk, but I interrupted him. I told him I needed to see him, that something terrible had happened, and that I couldn't talk about it over the phone. He agreed to meet me at a pizza place.

I felt like it took forever for him to come, but he finally showed up. He wanted to know what was wrong.

"You tell me what is wrong with you first," I said. I could tell he wasn't himself, but who would be under the circumstances and after all we had been through. I wasn't prepared for what he said to me.

He told me he felt like he wanted to have sex with me. He said Dad had told him he wanted all of us to have sex together. He also admitted he had planned to kill himself that night. I kept telling myself to be calm, not flip out, and be careful how I answered this. I nodded my head and then finally said, "I think we need to go and talk to a doctor, and if he says it's okay, then we will do it."

I will never know how I got him to agree to go with me to the hospital when we left the restaurant. All I can think of now is that it had to be God and the angels surrounding me that night. I got him to agree to let me drive him to the hospital, and when we got there, he told them everything. Needless to say, they admitted him.

One of the hardest things I had to do was tell my mom where he was and what he had planned to do. The facade of her perfect family had faded, and I guess she realized she could potentially lose another member of her family. My brother stayed in the hospital for a few days and was given an appointment to see a psychiatrist later that week.

The following week, my brother and sister-in-law started seeing a psychiatrist recommended by the hospital. The next thing I know, my brother calls me and says, "The doctor wants to see you. I told him about you and Dad."

I couldn't believe my ears because I didn't know my brother knew what had happened to me. After practically peeling myself off the floor, I asked him how he knew. Again, I wasn't prepared for what came next.

"I've known about it for years," he said. "Dad said you wanted it."

Dad said I wanted it? Did I hear this correctly? What eleven-year-old child wants to be molested and touched by a person they loved, respected, and deeply trusted? Again, a flood of emotions hit me. Anger, rage, and then: "Who else knows this?" I was told that my dad had told a distant uncle. So, I realized that at least two people knew and did nothing to stop, prevent, or protect me. How worthless can a person be made to feel? If I hadn't felt valued before, I certainly didn't feel like I was of any value now. I was furious with my brother for telling the doctor this and for never attempting to protect me or talk to me to see if what my dad had told him was true.

I did, however, start going to the psychiatrist three times a week. I can't remember much except that it was a place I could yell and scream and tell him how I hated my dad but loved him at the same time. None of it made any sense to me. My entire family made no sense to me. I couldn't understand how my brother could continue to live with my sister-in-law. All he would say was that if he left her, Dad's death would be in vain.

In the meantime, God was so merciful to me. I still had not shed a tear, and it was going on five months. I fell asleep one night and had a dream that I was sitting at a picnic table with my dad at the airport. A plane was sitting on the runway. He looked at me and said, "I will always love you, but you have to let me go." He walked up the stairs to the plane and waved goodbye. The plane took off, and I woke up screaming and crying. I sat for an entire day while the tears that had been bottled up for so long just flowed. I never knew someone could cry for so many hours. At the end of the day, I was exhausted and went to bed.

Things only got more chaotic, and I decided to take a trip to visit some old college friends I had made a few years earlier when I had been in West Palm Beach. The doctor agreed and said it was a good idea.

While I was gone, I called home, and my sister-in-law answered the phone. Laughingly, she said, "We got released from the doctor today. Now you are the only nut left in the family."

I remember telling her that it was a good thing there were a thousand miles between us because if I were there, I would kill her.

When I got home, I went straight to the doctor's office to ream him out. After I yelled at him, he calmly said, "Catherine, I can't help them. Your sister-in-law accepts no responsibility for what she has done."

Then I understood. It made perfect sense and helped me see that they were living in a state of denial, as was my mother.

I kept going to the doctor as I felt like my whole world was crashing around me, and he was the only one I could talk to. My mother acted like everything was normal, and my brother had no intention of leaving his wife. He didn't care how I felt or how my mother felt. He expected us to accept her, and that was it. What? Are you kidding me? I felt like they were all crazy and that I was the only sane one left in the family. I just couldn't stand to be around any of them.

Eventually, after many visits with the psychiatrist, I told him how I felt and that I had decided to move to Florida. I told him all I wanted to worry about was a roof over my head, food in my stomach, and an electric bill. He looked at me and said, "I have been waiting for you to make this decision." I told him it would be difficult, as I didn't think they would let me go. He said he would talk to my mother and make sure she would agree with it.

I called a family meeting and told them what I was planning to do. I even told my mother about how I had been molested and what had occurred with my grandfather. I watched her body language and facial expression to see if there was any hint that she had known but could not detect anything. She claimed she didn't know, but deep inside of me, I wondered. My brother was furious with me when I told him my plan. He wanted to know how I could do this to them after all they had been through. I told him we had all been through the same thing, but we were all dealing with it in different ways. He said he would never forgive me, and he left. My mother said she understood and that the doctor told her that if she didn't let me go, she would be visiting me at the grave.

Shortly after the family meeting, I was determined to get out of there ASAP. I called one of my friends and told him what I was planning to do. He offered to fly to New Orleans and help me drive to Tampa. Back in those days, it was a twelve-hour drive, and that was without stopping. He was living with his mom at the time and invited me to come and stay with them until I could get a job and get my own place. All he knew at the time was that my dad had committed suicide and I had to get away from my family. I was unable to tell him the rest of the story.

My friend came and we made the trip. All I packed in my car were dishes, clothes, and some pots and pans. The day we left New Orleans, a huge weight lifted off me as we drove across the bridge. Freedom. Freedom from living every day on edge, waiting for the next crisis to surface, freedom from being told how I should feel, freedom from manipulation and control, and freedom from the guilt that my brother had tried to put on me for leaving. He told me he would never forgive me for leaving, but I was so *done* I didn't care.

"Twisted and perverse lives are surrounded by demonic influence.
If you value your soul, stay far away from them."
– Proverbs 22:5 (TPT)

Chapter

FOUR

A FEW MONTHS AFTER MY DAD DIED, I packed everything I could fit in my car and moved to Tampa, Florida. I was twenty-one years old. It was the beginning of 1972, and I had arranged to stay with friends until I could find a job and get on my feet. I had occasionally worked in my dad's business, answering the phone and as an information operator for a short time. Other than that, I had no skills, but I didn't care. Anything would be better than living with a family who was half-crazy. I wanted some normalcy in my life, but I didn't even know what that would look like. I was so wounded and wondered if things would ever get any better.

Eventually, I found a job as a receptionist at a diesel engine company. The president's secretary interviewed me and asked if I could type. I told her yes. When you're desperate, you will do anything to get a job. As I look back, it was God who gave me that job through her. Quickly, she discovered I couldn't type, so she brought me a typing book and an old typewriter to take home and practice on. She was kind enough to keep my secret while I taught myself to type. I made seventy-two dollars a week. Even in those days, that was not much money.

I eventually got my own place and bought a waterbed with no frame for twenty-seven dollars. I had my waterbed on the floor, no furniture, boxes with my clothes in them, and a few pots for cooking. The words I had spoken to the psychiatrist had come to pass. I had an electric bill and rent to pay but no telephone. At that point, a phone was a luxury I couldn't afford. I had all I could mentally deal with.

I would call home—collect—once every six weeks or so from a pay phone or a friend's home. On one of those calls, I found out that my mother had moved in with my brother and his wife. Another shock. Later, I learned that she was taking care of his house and kids while he and his wife worked. My mother kept saying she was doing it for the kids.

I lived in Florida for three years, and during that time, my mother only came to see me twice. She came with my sister-in-law and the three kids. The message I got from this was that I wasn't worth much for her to take the time to spend with me alone. I was glad when they left. The phone calls were fewer and fewer after that because all I would hear about was what was going on in the family.

Things for me weren't much better. I had met this guy and really fell for him. He was so good-looking, kind, and sweet. He had been in the military and dishonorably discharged, but what did I know about a dishonorable discharge? He told me it was because he wouldn't follow their orders.

I quickly learned that the problem with him was that he was looking for someone to take care of him. He lived with his parents and wouldn't work. He thought we would get together and I would support him. That didn't last. I needed someone to support me and care for me. After that, I stayed to myself. I wasn't eager to venture out again and find another disaster. I figured it was better to be alone and at peace than to go through more drama. I was looking for love, not understanding that I needed healing first.

I ended up leaving Florida due to injuring my back when I fell through a pier onto a dry beach. A friend drove me home, and because I couldn't work, I had to move into my brother's house. I would have rather been homeless, but they wouldn't have it any other way. As soon as possible, I got a job, found an apartment, and moved out. Living with seven people in a three-bedroom, one-bath home is difficult enough without all the underlying tension.

My mother decided to move in with me, giving some excuse that she couldn't let me live alone. Where was she during the three years I lived alone in Florida, I wondered. Well, again, no furniture. Just a mattress on the floor. My brother was very angry with me. He couldn't believe I would bring our mother to live under those conditions. I quickly reminded him she was an adult and then asked if he was afraid that he would lose his babysitter and housekeeper. That certainly didn't win any points with him.

Then I understood. It made perfect sense
and helped me see that they were living in
a state of denial, as was my mother.

My relationship with my brother deteriorated into a love-hate situation. Perhaps it was because of finding out how he had known about the abuse for years and never did anything to help me. Or maybe it was that I felt he was shoving this woman he was married to down our throats, forcing us to accept her whether we liked it or not. He seemed so selfish to me. It was always about him, his life, his problems, and his wants, needs, and desires. Everyone seemed to cater to him, especially my mother.

After moving in with me, she continued to get up every morning and go to his house to be his chief cook and bottle washer. This went on for a month or so until I finally sat her down and said, "This has to stop." She was shocked.

I told her I had found out about a school where she could learn basic skills like typing, bookkeeping, and clerical work. I told her it was a twelve-month program, and at the end, they would help her find a job. They also paid a small stipend while she was in school. Amazingly, she agreed to do it.

After she was accepted into the program, she had my brother come over to tell him about it. Well, World War III hit. He began yelling and saying things like, "Dad didn't want you working! I will not allow this!"

I looked at him and said, "She isn't ninety years old in a wheelchair. She is forty-five years old and still has a lot of living to do." My parents had married when she was fifteen and my dad was seventeen. My mother was widowed at age forty-two and had never worked a day in her life. This put another wedge between my brother and me, as Mom would no longer be going to his house every day to do his housework.

This was the '70s when women were waking up and taking charge of their lives. The song by Helen Reddy, "I Am Woman," was my favorite song then because I had built walls to tell myself I was the only one I could depend on and trust and that I would take care of myself and my mother.

After she graduated, she got a job with a government agency as a purchasing agent. This gave her confidence, and my brother started to see the change in her. He told me I had created a monster. I wanted to scream at him: "No, you are a monster! A sick, perverted monster who feels like everyone should cater to you at any expense."

I didn't have much to do with him, but we did have to continue the traditional holidays with his family. There were times I felt like my food would get stuck in my throat. My mother had managed to piece her family back together in her mind, but in reality, togetherness was the farthest thing from the truth. Again, she made her world what she wanted it to be. She wouldn't accept that the two of us weren't close and probably never would be.

During this time, my mother started seeing a chiropractor for her back problems. When she would come home and tell me about her appointments, I sensed that this man was interested in her. I asked her what she would do if he asked her to go out for coffee. She got very nervous and said, "There was only one man for me, and that was your father."

How could she continue to think about the man who caused so much grief and pain to everyone around him? I told her this could be a fresh start for her and that not all men were like my dad.

"There will never be another man in my life," she said.

Sure enough, her chiropractor asked her out for coffee at her next appointment. She declined and never went back to see him. This was so sad to me, as I felt like she could have had a chance at some semblance of happiness.

In the meantime, my brother told us he was taking his family and moving to Indianapolis. He felt they all needed a fresh start. My mother was upset, as she wasn't going to see the grandchildren like she had been able to. Not long after that, he sold his house and moved.

My mother and I went up to see them for Christmas, and it was the coldest winter they had had in a hundred years. I thought he had lost his mind for moving to a place where the snow was up to the second-story windows. I had never experienced that kind of deep-cutting cold. It was good to see the kids, but I was glad when we got home.

My brother lived there for about three years before another phone call came with another crisis. His wife had moved out of the house, taking the middle child and leaving my oldest niece and my nephew, the baby of the family, with my brother. She had had another affair and ran off with one of my brother's best friends. My mother asked me to take the only vacation I had that year and drive up to help them pack; then, after ten days, she would drive up and finish packing to move them back.

I couldn't refuse. All I could think about was my niece and nephew. They were young when everything happened the first time, but they were older now and would understand what was going on. My niece was twelve, and my nephew was nine. I couldn't imagine what it felt like having your own mother desert you.

When I arrived, the house was a disaster. My sister-in-law had never been a good housekeeper, but this was beyond anything I had ever seen. I couldn't open the laundry room door because the clothes were piled up to the door-knob. The laundry room was not small—it was bigger than a walk-in closet. From the time I arrived there, I washed, cooked, and packed from morning until night. My brother would come home, and at dinner, we would all sit at the table to eat, but no one spoke.

My nephew wouldn't eat and would ask to be excused. Every night, he would leave the table, and then around nine o'clock, he would come and ask me to fix him something to eat. I knew he just couldn't sit at the table with all of us to eat, so I kept his plate on the side and would heat it up later and sit with him while he ate. My niece and nephew never showed any emotion and didn't want to talk about what had happened. I couldn't blame them.

I couldn't imagine having your mother walk out, leave you, and take your sister with her. The feelings they were experiencing were painful to watch. When your own mother rejects you, it is one of the deepest wounds a human being can experience.

My mom showed up ten days later as I was preparing to go back to work. She looked around and asked me what I had been doing, insinuating that I had not done anything while I had been there. My niece came to my rescue, telling her what a disaster it had been and that I had worked from morning to night. As for my brother, he had checked out completely. He never really talked to the kids or me the whole time I was there. This only angered me even more because, as usual, it was what he was going through, and it was all about him and his feelings and emotions, forgetting his children were hurting, too. He was an emotional cripple.

They all came back to New Orleans, and my mother moved in with them to take care of the kids. My brother decided he needed another wife, so he spent all of his free time hitting the dating scene.

I would frequently go to see my mom, niece, and nephew. My brother was busy working and rarely home. When he wasn't working, he was dating and going out with his friends. This left my niece and nephew at home alone with my mom. It infuriated me how he just left them to my mom to raise. He was a good provider, but that's not what they needed. They needed and craved his attention.

Kids are resilient, but why should they have to be? I used to tell him about that song by Harry Chapin. My brother was like the character in the song. The little boy would ask his father when he was coming home. The dad's response was "Not today," and he would give a litany of reasons why he couldn't come home. At the end of the song, the dad asks when his son is coming to visit him, and the son's response is "Not today," and he would give reasons why he wasn't coming.

"This will be your life," I told my brother. "You only have one chance with your kids, and you are throwing it away."

They were great kids! I loved them, and they loved me. Later, when my niece was old enough, she would marry to get out of the house. My nephew was pretty closed off most of his life. Who could blame him?

My brother finally settled down and found two women he was interested in. We met both, and naturally, the one we liked and hoped he would marry, he didn't. Instead, he married the woman we didn't particularly care for. She was his type, an airhead who waited on him hand and foot and who would let him get by with anything. His idea of marriage was to have a woman serve him, cook for him, clean for him, and let him do whatever he wanted to do.

As the years went by and we spent holidays with them, she always picked a fight with him. Christmas and Thanksgiving were, again, never peaceful. We would be invited for dinner, and the tension would be unbearable; another meal where my food would get caught in my throat.

She tried to put a wedge between him and us. Finally, I told my mother, "No more! I'm not spending another holiday with them."

Again, everyone got along in my mother's world. You just didn't rock the boat.

Chapter

FIVE

BY THE MID-SEVENTIES, I was living in Baton Rouge, still trying to get my life together. I was twenty-four years old and dating an attorney I was in love with. I had moved to Baton Rouge to be with him, and we moved in together. I was with him for three years before I discovered that he didn't want to get married or have any children.

During this time, God was trying to get my attention. One night, I had a dream. My boyfriend and I were in a big building where people were sitting at long tables, looking intently at large open books. They looked up at us and said, "Today is the day. Today is the day the world is going to end."

Suddenly, a bright light came down all around us. The light then began to rise, and as I watched, people were going up into the light while we were still on the ground. I looked at him and said, "We missed it."

"Missed what?" he asked.

"I don't know," I said, "but we missed it."

We walked outside the building, and a wall of fire came at us. That's when I woke up. The dream seemed so real that I bolted out of bed and ran out the front door. I was terrified. I looked around outside and realized it was still night, so I came back inside the house.

That morning, I told my boyfriend about the dream. He told me I could talk to him about these things but to never talk about them to anyone else, as they would think I was crazy. I began to question him.

"We need to get married," I said. "How can you be a deacon in your church and be living in sin with me?"

It kept eating at me, so I packed his clothes and had them waiting at the door for him one night. We argued, and I told him someone would come along that I would only know for a short time and that I would marry him. I told him he would be left high and dry and all alone. He left. Little did I know at the time that those words would come to pass.

Not long after, I went out one night, partying and drinking. On the way home, I was in a horrible automobile accident. I drove my car off a cliff, and it flipped end over end seven times with me inside of it. It was late at night, and I was at the bottom of a cliff. Thank God there were people behind me, and they called the police. It took the rescue team two hours to cut me out of the car, going through the windshield with the Jaws of Life. I was unconscious but remember coming to and seeing flashing red lights. I heard a voice yell, "She's alive!"

I passed out again and came to in the emergency room. I looked down and saw my wrist bone sticking through the flesh of my right arm. I didn't feel any pain and asked them to hurry and stitch me up because I had to work the next morning. The next thing I knew, I woke up riding on a gurney as they took me to my room. It was three o'clock in the morning, and I kept telling them I had to go to work. They just laughed at me.

I woke up the next day in the hospital with a cast on my right arm, a sling on my left arm, and an IV running. I called for the nurse to help me go to the bathroom. She came in with a bedpan. I told her I didn't need that, but I almost passed out when I tried to stand up. I told the nurse that if it took all day, I was going to the bathroom at the foot of my bed. It took a while for me to get there. My whole body felt like I had been through a meat grinder.

When I passed in front of the mirror, I caught a glimpse of my face. I had two black eyes and a gash over my forehead. The rest of my body was black and blue from my neck down to my knees. My mother came and told me that everyone who had ever crashed there had died instantly. The police told her I was the only person who had ever survived a wreck in that spot. In the back of my mind, I wondered, "Why am I still here? What purpose could I possibly have for still being alive?"

Now, as I look back, I realize that God was beginning to call me. I began to think about the dream I had and how I felt convicted for living with a man and not being married to him. I couldn't understand how he could be a deacon in his church and live the way we were living.

After I was discharged from the hospital, my mother took me to see the car I had been driving that night. I couldn't believe my eyes. The car was totally crushed. It was lying on its roof when they got to me. My body was sideways on the ceiling of the car when they cut me out of it. I was living alone and had a lot of time to think. I was afraid. I didn't want to be alone, yet I knew I couldn't go back to living with my boyfriend. I returned to work a week later and was still pondering what had occurred.

Not long after, a dear friend called me out of the blue. We had gone to high school together and dated for a brief time before college. He was voted "Most Likely to Succeed" by our classmates, had been captain of the football team, and president of his fraternity. He lived in New Orleans and told me his wife had had an affair, and he left her. It amazed me how we could just pick up right where we had left off. That's how it is when you have a good friend.

I had always had a crush on him through school and had hoped that we would get married. Eventually, we both went away to college, him to a school in northern Louisiana, and me, briefly, to Florida. We kept in touch for a while. He dropped out of college, and then when I came back, we dated again but not for long. He married someone else, and I was devastated but didn't show it. I was so good at hiding my feelings.

My family knew my friend, too. As a matter of fact, at one point, while I was in Baton Rouge, he was working for my brother. He eventually bought my brother's business from him. My family liked him, so when they found out we were seeing each other again, they were happy about it.

When my brother remarried, my mother went to live with them. I was still in Baton Rouge. I had stopped seeing the attorney. Looking back, I think he was hurt by what his ex-wife had done to him, and I was hurt by ending a three-year relationship. I was tired of trying to find love, and I wanted a baby and a stable life. I wanted to settle down and have a family, a home, and some security.

I moved back to New Orleans, and within a month, we were married. I was twenty-eight years old and thrilled, thinking, "This is it! I have someone who loves me for me and who will take care of me!"

My husband had no idea of my history of abuse or my family's history. Those were details I never discussed with anyone. I didn't want people's views of me to be tainted by the perversion and total dysfunction I had lived through. Those were dark, walled places in my heart that were sealed and never to be opened. I put a lid on them, neatly shoving them all away, not realizing there would come a day when they would spill out into a life I was trying to keep together. Believe me, I was no angel. I was full of fear. I was drinking and partying, trying to dull the pain I felt inside, yet smiling and functioning on the outside.

In the beginning, life with my husband was good, but it quickly began to change. I discovered that the man of my dreams was an alcoholic. He had two small children from his first marriage, and we were in the process of filing for custody of them when I noticed his drinking had intensified. I attributed it to the drama we were going through with the custody fight. His ex-wife had been dealing drugs, and we had so much evidence on her that it only took three days in court for us to win.

Overnight, I became a mother of two little boys from his previous marriage. I was excited and thought, "Now that the case is over, he'll settle down, and we will raise a family together." How wrong I was. His drinking escalated along with his staying out all night, not working the business he owned, and not paying the bills. We began having horrible screaming matches. The anger and rage I had managed to stuff all those years came out every time we fought. I was vicious, lashing out at him because he wasn't living up to my expectations.

Soon, I realized I was in another mess. My life was the definition of "in the toilet." My marriage of not even a year was a disaster. I was at the end of myself, miserable, depressed, and on the brink of suicide.

When a neighbor of my brother's invited me to go to a Bible study with her, I remember thinking, "Well, I've tried everything else." I thought about the Bible stories I had heard when I was in high school and how peaceful I felt in those classes. I also started to think about what I had been through when I lived in Baton Rouge, my dream, the accident, and the chaos of my life. I was so desperate and felt so alone. I wondered if anything in my pathetic life would ever get any better. So, I said, "Sure, why not?"

On a Wednesday night, my husband came home early, and I asked him to watch the kids so I could go. I think he was glad for me to leave the house because of all the fighting we had been doing. My brother's neighbor picked me up, and we went together. We drove up to this big house in an affluent part of town. Cars were lined all up and down the street. The house was lit up, and when we rang the bell, a petite, dark-haired lady answered and invited us in. She kindly introduced herself as Mary and then introduced us to everyone else. Mary was especially cordial, and I felt comfortable with her.

Everyone was seated and talking amongst themselves. A couple who sat in the front were ministers from a church I had never heard of or been to. I hadn't stepped foot inside a church in about fifteen years, so this was totally new to me. The ministers began to teach on scriptures from the Bible. I was hearing things I had never heard before and was drawn, almost mesmerized, by what they were teaching. I felt a peace I hadn't felt in a long time, not since that Bible course I took in high school. I felt like I was drinking a long, cold drink of water. It was washing through me, and I wanted more.

That was where I met Jesus Christ. Most people can tell you the day and the hour they met the Lord, but not me. It was a process. I was invited back, and when I left that night, I knew I would return. I needed whatever it was that was there.

The following week, I called my brother's neighbor to see about going to the meeting with her, and she told me she wasn't going to go back. She gave no reason as to why, and I didn't ask. I thought it was strange, though, because there was such peace there. I couldn't understand how anyone would not want that. I didn't care if she went or not; I just knew they had something that I desperately needed. I felt hope there, and the people all had problems but appeared to be genuinely happy. It was so refreshing. My soul had thirsted for this feeling without knowing what it needed. I went back every Wednesday night and got to know everyone there.

I left each meeting with hope that life would get better, and then I would get home, and reality would hit. There were times when I would get home, and we would start fighting the minute I walked in the door because my husband would be drunk. I would go upstairs and lock the bedroom door and read my Bible. That's when the Word became alive to me. That's when I began to see that I could trust Jesus and what His Word said. I began to see who He was.

> *"This is why I tell you to never be worried about your life, for all that you need will be provided, such as food, water, clothing—everything your body needs. Isn't there more to your life than a meal? Isn't your body more than clothing? Consider the birds—do you think they worry about their existence? They don't plant or reap or store up food, yet your heavenly Father provides them each with food. Aren't you much more valuable to your Father than they? So, which one of you by worrying could add anything to your life?"*
> – Matthew 6:25–27 (TPT)

I was trying to decide what to do about my marriage. I knew if the drinking didn't stop, I wouldn't be able to stay, yet I also knew what God thought about divorce. I was struggling with what to do. I was also worried about taking care of myself since I didn't have much work experience.

I continued to be faithful in going to the Bible study every week. I would count the days until the next Bible study, and many times, I would be crying while driving there. I would get there, wipe my face, and walk into the arms of Jesus. No one there knew what I was going through. I never talked about my problems or told them what was happening at home. My husband wasn't interested in going, and I never encouraged him much, as this was a place of refuge for me. This was a place where there was healing, deliverance, and restoration.

Eventually, Mary started a ladies' prayer group. We met on Friday nights at her house. In that prayer group, God began to really work on me. The things of my life that I had buried deep inside began to surface. I had never trusted anyone and never shared anything with anyone about my life. I had promised myself that those dark things would never be spoken of or looked at again. Not by me or anyone else.

After about a year of going to the Bible study and prayer group, I was at Mary's one morning. It was just the two of us in the kitchen talking. Out of nowhere, I began to tell her about my life. I remember the look on her face, which she quickly tried to hide. It was a look of shock, sadness, and compassion. I tried to change the subject and shove what I was feeling back down, but I couldn't. Everything just came tumbling out. I don't remember much of what happened after that. All I can say is that because of that morning, I was able to trust again.

I felt safe with Mary—I knew she would keep my deepest, darkest secrets—and best of all, there was no judgment. I had always been afraid of being judged for all the junk I had been through, but not with Mary. We became close friends. This woman poured out her life for me. I used to call her "The General" because she could pray heaven down, and the power of God would manifest, and demons would flee!

Meanwhile, I still struggled in my marriage. Aside from my concerns about the morality of divorce and how I would take care of myself without a husband, one of the deepest desires of my heart was to have a family. I wanted a child of my own. I felt that if I left my marriage, I would never marry again.

Yet, in reading the Bible, I would come across scriptures like Matthew 7:7–11, where Jesus says ask and it shall be given to you, seek and you will find. I began to ask God, "This is what Your Word says. Is it true? Will you take care of me? Will you provide for me?" Again, more scriptures were revealed to me, always encouraging me to step out on faith and trust Him.

I decided to take things into my own hands. I went to my OB-GYN doctor and obtained fertility pills. I wanted a family, whether this marriage was going to work or not. I started taking the medication, and not long after starting, I reached for them one morning and thought I heard God speak to me. This was the first time I could really hear His voice. He said, "Throw those away. I'm sending you a child, and it will be very soon."

I stopped, looked at the bottle, and thought, "I'm going to trust what I'm hearing," and threw them in the trash. I was twenty-nine years old. This was in February 1980. It's funny how some dates just stick in your mind while others escape you.

> "Ask, and the gift is yours. Seek, and you'll discover. Knock, and the
> door will be opened for you. For every persistent one will get what
> he asks for. Every persistent seeker will discover what he longs for.
> And everyone who knocks persistently will one day find an open
> door. Do you know of any parent who would give his hungry child,
> who asked for food, a plate of rocks instead? Or when asked for a
> piece of fish, what parent would offer his child a snake instead? If
> you, imperfect as you are. know how to lovingly take care of your
> children and give them what's best, how much more ready is your
> heavenly Father to give wonderful gifts to those who ask him?"
> – Matthew 7:7–11 (TPT)

PART TWO

Finding Father

Chapter
SIX

MY HUSBAND AND I continued having our ups and downs. I wasn't fighting with him as much because I was spending more time in my Bible and finding peace amidst all the turmoil. I had gone to a pastor to ask him about divorce. He would never give me a straight answer. I was torn. I only wanted to do what God would allow me to do.

I also told God that if He was going to send me a child, it would have to be by immaculate conception, as my husband was staying out just about every night. His mother would babysit on the day I went to Bible study. I was learning about God and trying to be as good as I could. I wanted to do what He wanted me to do. I didn't want to make any hasty decisions.

> One of the best qualities of the Lord is that He meets you right where you are. He sits with you right in the mud pit of life and waits for you to ask Him for help.

He waits for you to ask Him for help, and then He starts to show you ever so gently. It is amazing how patient and gentle He is. You begin to give Him your heart and ask Him to take over your life. I was learning His word, and it gave me peace and comfort. I was learning through His Word, which would speak to me, and it would be relevant to what was happening at the time.

May rolled around, and a flood came. We were stuck in the house for three days. My husband couldn't leave, as there was no way out. The streets were underwater, which was up to our door but never came into the house. That was when God sent my daughter to me.

When I was three months pregnant, I told my husband, and he seemed genuinely happy. He kept saying he would stop drinking but never did. When I was six months pregnant, he came home drunk one night, and he had a friend with him—at least that's what I was told. I thought this man was an old friend from college. My husband passed out on the couch, and then I discovered the man was a hitchhiker my husband had picked up on the side of the road. The two boys were asleep upstairs, my husband was passed out on the sofa, and I had no telephone, as it had been cut off.

This man told me he had left his family in Michigan and hitchhiked down to Louisiana to look for work. My husband had picked him up, offered him a job, and told him he could stay with us. I was terrified at the thought of my husband being passed out and me being basically alone with this hitch-hiker. What was my husband thinking?

My patience was wearing thin. That night, I got in my car and drove to my brother's house. It was late, and I didn't want to wake anyone, so I slept in the car in front of his house. I prayed and prayed that God would show me what to do. I was worried about leaving, wondering who would take care of the boys.

I went home the next day, and when I confronted my husband about what he had done, I was told that I was pregnant, I was stuck, and I just had to take whatever he dished out because no one would hire me. He had told this man that he and his family could move in with us. I talked to the man's wife that evening and told her not to come because we had marital problems, and I didn't want her moving in with us.

Two weeks later, she showed up with two children on my doorstep. I couldn't believe the audacity of this woman. The next day, I watched my husband and this man pull out of the driveway and leave for work. I picked up the phone, which had finally been turned on, called my family, and told them I was leaving him. Everyone showed up, and I was packed and out of a three-bedroom house within six hours. I took the boys to my mother-in-law and told her I was leaving.

The hitchhiker's wife sat on the floor, watching me pack everything up and load the truck. I called every storage place in town, but no one had a vacancy. A woman at the last place I called said she had a waiting list. I told her, "Ma'am, I'm six months pregnant, and I have to leave my husband today."

The woman said, "Come on. I have a vacancy and will put you at the top of the list."

My mother was loading up the last of the folding chairs she had given me when the hitchhiker's wife told her the chairs belonged to her. Dumbfounded, my mother told the woman, "No, these chairs belong to my daughter. I know because I gave them to her."

I couldn't believe this woman had the nerve to lie and try to insinuate herself into my circumstance. We loaded up everything that had belonged to me before we got married. I left him with his refrigerator, bed, and dining room table. Needless to say, I was relieved when we left.

That night, I got on a plane, flew to Atlanta, Georgia, and stayed with a friend until it was time for me to deliver my baby. I thought I would have heard from my husband, but I didn't. It was evident that our marriage was over. I didn't file for a divorce at that time. I just wanted to get my life back on track.

In January of 1981, I flew back to New Orleans to await the birth of my baby. My mother had found government-subsidized housing—the projects—for us to live in. The apartment was nine hundred square feet and in a decent area of the city, so life was getting a little better. In the meantime, I continued going to Bible study, and God was becoming more real to me every day.

When my mother and I moved into the apartment, we had no telephone. My mother had a job. With no job, no education, and very little experience, I was on state assistance with food stamps. All I could afford was food and a roof over my head.

My husband and I had not talked, and he didn't give me any financial support during my pregnancy. During this time, I discovered through the grapevine that he had given a woman he was running with a thousand dollars and set her up in an apartment. I was devastated. I couldn't understand how he could be so callous and just ignore the fact that he had a child coming into this world. One night, while I was waiting for the Bible study to start, I opened my Bible and it fell open to 1 Timothy 5:8. "But if anyone does not provide for his relatives, and especially for members of his household, he has denied the faith and is worse than an unbeliever." *(ESV)*

I was shocked and comforted, as I knew God was watching over me. He knew the pain and hurt I was feeling and showed me that He is ever-knowing and present in every situation of my life. I realized He was with me. I felt His sweet presence the entire time I carried my daughter, and I had great peace. I didn't know how it all would work out, and it saddened me greatly to think about how my husband never attempted to talk to me about the upcoming birth of our child. We hadn't even talked about divorce. We just never communicated about anything. After that night, whenever I heard something about my husband, I would recite that scripture and say, "That's okay. He's going to burn in hell for eternity." God was gracious to me in spite of the bitterness that was taking root in my heart.

One thing I know and remember vividly is that I was on cloud nine the entire time I was pregnant. God was with me every step of the way. His presence was undeniable. His comfort, love, and provision were more than I had ever dreamed possible. I wished I could have lived in that state for the rest of my life. It was so precious and so profound. I was literally wrapped in a cocoon of His love. He carried me every day.

The way He took care of me was better than having a husband. On one occasion, I was craving shrimp so badly but didn't have the money to buy any. My brother called me and invited me to dinner at his house. When I got there, I asked what we were having. He said he didn't know but that whatever it was, his wife had it in the fridge. When I opened the door, there was a gigantic bowl of big raw shrimp. I started crying. My brother chalked it up to being hormonal, but I knew God was giving me my heart's desire and loving me so much that He gave me what I wanted and needed.

Driving to the grocery store one day, I asked the Lord to help me get a phone. I reasoned that if I were alone when I went into labor, I might need to call for help. He instantly told me to go to the phone company. I argued with Him and told Him they wanted a one-hundred-dollar deposit, and I didn't have a hundred dollars. Again, the still, small voice said, "Go to the phone company."

Frustrated, I answered, "Okay. I will go and humiliate myself and tell them I don't have a hundred dollars for the deposit."

Little did I know how God was setting me up for a big surprise. I drove to the phone company and walked in. It was strange because a woman approached me and asked how she could help me, and it felt like I had two hands on my shoulders as I sidestepped the woman without answering and walked straight to the back of the store and stood there. Another woman came up to me and asked how she could help. I remember saying, "As you can see, I am about ready to have this baby, and I need a phone."

She looked at me and said, "I think I know you. Didn't you work for the phone company?" I had worked for the phone company twelve years before and had not even thought about that. I didn't recognize her, but she recognized me. We had worked together.

She smiled and said, "Here," and handed me a phone. "I'll have it turned on today. Just don't make any long-distance calls." She did not mention a deposit.

I was stunned. I gratefully took the phone and drove home in tears, asking God to forgive me for not trusting Him. I had a phone that worked and didn't have to pay the required deposit. When was I going to learn not to argue with Him? He is the Maker of the universe. Wouldn't He know how to give me a phone?

Again, He was showing me His provision for me with great love and patience. I was learning how to trust Him with each trial I faced, and my faith was growing because of it.

A few days later, I went into labor at five o'clock in the morning. I had to call my mom, who was already at work, and ask her to come and get me and take me to the hospital. After eighteen long hours of labor, my beautiful daughter, Amanda, was born. It was the happiest, most satisfying day of my life. She was beautiful but very sick. During labor, I spiked a high fever of 105 degrees, and when she was born, I heard the doctor say, "I want cultures on the cord stat." I looked over and saw that she was blue and barely moving. I began to ask questions and instantly felt a burning in my hand, and then I was out.

I woke up the next morning, asking where my baby was and asking to see her. The nurses kept putting me off, which made me wonder what they were hiding. Finally, the doctor came in and told me she had been born septic and was in the intensive care unit on intravenous antibiotics. He told me they wanted to do a spinal tap to see if the infection had gone to her brain. I didn't have the presence of mind to ask questions. Reluctantly, I gave them permission.

I had the peace that surpasses all understanding. God had been with me the entire time. He carried me through my pregnancy and delivery. I trusted Him and felt He would take care of this, and He did. When the results came back, they were negative. The infection had not crossed the blood-brain barrier, but she had to remain in the hospital for ten days to be treated. We were isolated from the rest of the mothers, and I was also on antibiotics. The hardest thing I had to do was leave the hospital without my beautiful baby. I had to get a ride every day to the hospital to see her and feed her, as I was not allowed to drive.

Her father never came to the hospital to see her. My mother had called his mother and told her about the delivery and all the complications. No one from his family came. I was hurt by all that had occurred and needed time to adjust to being a mother.

Finally, after ten days, my brother took me to the hospital, and we brought my daughter home. I was thrilled but scared because I was alone. My mom had come down with the flu and couldn't be near us. When my brother left, there I sat with this beautiful baby, not knowing what I was supposed to do. After a few hours, I changed her diaper and saw blood in it. I panicked. I called the ICU and hysterically told them I was bringing her back. Calmly, the nurse asked me what was wrong. I told her about the blood. She reassured me that sometimes this happens and that it's from a hormone that the baby releases. I was relieved, to say the least.

That was my first night alone with her. After that, I settled into knowing I was responsible for her and would fight heaven and earth to keep her safe and secure. I never knew the depth of love I would have for her until after she was born.

Chapter
SEVEN

SETTLING INTO MOTHERHOOD, I realized I had to think about how I would provide for my daughter. I had to get a job or a career. I couldn't count on her dad, as we still weren't on speaking terms.

Growing up, I had always wanted to be a candy striper at the local hospital. I had a dream of being a doctor or a nurse one day, but my dad, being Italian, wouldn't hear of it. No woman in his family would ever be allowed to work in that kind of environment. He thought it wasn't very dignified.

Well, he was gone, and now I had to figure out how I would take care of this tiny person who was dependent on me. I found out about a surgical technician program at Charity Hospital. It only took a year to complete, and then you could be certified to work in surgery in any hospital anywhere. I felt like that was quick and would give me a skill to support us. When my daughter was two years old, I enrolled.

I was getting a small check from the state, living on food stamps, and the school paid a small stipend each month while I was studying and working in the hospital. I had to be at the hospital at six thirty every morning. My mother would take my daughter to daycare for me, as no daycare opened before 6:00 a.m. She was a tremendous help to me, and I will always be grateful for what she did.

The program was grueling. The pressure and stress were incredible. Some of the people had worked there for eons. They were state workers and couldn't be fired. Hence, they could pretty much get away with anything.

I remember an incident where I was setting up for a case and the circulator was being so rude and obnoxious. She yelled and cursed at me. Enraged, I reached for the scalpel. I was going to stab her. Then I whispered, "Jesus." Instantly, it was like warm oil began to flow over me; the rage turned into incredible peace. I began to smile behind my mask. She noticed and became even more enraged. She started screaming like a banshee and ran out of the room. She never came back, which was fine with me.

That year, I scrubbed on all kinds of cases. Brain tumors, burn victims, broken hips, automobile accidents—you name it, and I saw it. One of the instructors told me that when I left there, I would say I missed that place.

"Never," I said. "I will be so glad to leave."

Well, she was right. After leaving, I did miss it. I missed the chaos, the cases, the doctors, and the staff. One of the other students said she had been in nursing school at Charity and had to drop out because it was too hard. I remember looking at her and asking, "Is it harder than this?"

She smiled and said, "No. That was a piece of cake compared to this program."

After a year, I graduated and got a part-time job at one of the local hospitals. They didn't have a full-time position available, but I took it to get my foot in the door, and it was only three miles from where I lived. I had to take calls during the week and on some weekends. That was good, as it was extra money on my paycheck.

I continued to be involved in the Bible study and intercessory prayer group. They were supportive and prayed over us just about every week. My prayer group and my dear friend Mary kept encouraging me to go to nursing school. Little did they know of the demons I constantly fought. Voices in my head told me how stupid I was, how I couldn't make it, and how inadequate I was.

One morning, Mary told me she kept seeing me with a nurse's hat on my head when we would pray. I told her she was dreaming, as that wasn't going to happen. I told her I had no intention of going back to school. I hated school, and being a surgical technician was all I could handle.

Then one day, while praying with our group, I had a vision. It was like I was out in space, looking at the world. It was in color, and it was breathtaking. I watched it slowly spinning, and then I heard the Lord say, "What if I would have said that I would not go?" I knew what He was saying. What if He had told the Father that He would not go and lay down His life for the world? What would have happened?

I didn't say anything to anyone, but in my car on the way home, I broke down in tears. I began to tell the Lord my thoughts:

"You have the wrong person."

"Don't you remember how bad I was in school? I can't do this!"

"What about Amanda? How will I take care of her?"

"I don't have any money. That takes money."

Every argument I could think of, I was shouting it out.

"You can't ask me to do this! Get someone else!"

"Face it. I'm stupid!"

No response. He just let me cry and shout about it. I drove around for a while, as my car was my prayer closet. Our apartment was small, and I didn't want anyone to hear me.

That night, I had a dream. In the dream, I was sitting at a table and Jesus walked up and sat down.

"Do you trust Me?" He asked.

"Yes," I answered.

"Then don't worry about money or Amanda," He said. "I will take care of them by my Spirit."

He smiled and left. Mary called me the next day and said she had a word for me from the Lord. She had written it down, and it was everything He had told me in my dream and more. How could I say no? I figured if I could make it in tech school, I could make it in nursing.

After more tears and great fear, I began gathering the information I needed to start. Remembering the girl who said Charity's nursing school was a piece of cake compared to the surgical tech program, I decided to continue my education there. It was a three-year diploma program and is world-renowned because Charity is the trauma hospital for the state of Louisiana. The training is hands-on, with students running the hospital and caring for all the patients. Once you graduate from there, you can get a job anywhere in the world.

When my daughter was almost three years old, we were riding in the car one day when she saw a picture of a man on a billboard.

"Mommy, is that my daddy?" she asked.

I didn't think I would have to deal with that for a long time, but I was wrong. I told her no and asked if she wanted to meet her daddy, and she said yes.

I had waited until after my daughter was born to file for divorce so she would not be illegitimate. Several months after her birth, the paperwork was finalized, and we were no longer married. When I called my ex-husband and told him she wanted to meet him, we agreed to meet at the park.

She vividly recalls her first memory of seeing him. He was sitting under a tree. The meeting went well, and we were civil to each other. After that, he saw her occasionally but nothing consistent. I would sometimes call him to come and see her or take her to the park because she would ask for him. Sometimes, he would say he was coming and then not show up. I could tell this hurt her, and I would try to alleviate her pain by saying, "Let's go shoe shopping." She would get excited and forget all about him not coming. (To this day, she *really* loves shoes!)

Once I made plans to go to nursing school, I decided to go to court to file for child support. I felt he should at least help with the cost of daycare. I filed papers with the child enforcement division and got a notice that we were going to court. I couldn't help but feel hopeful that the court would make him pay some kind of support. That was short-lived, as I got another notice saying it was postponed.

I was so angry that I asked my mother to babysit, got in my car, and went for a drive. Whenever I needed to pray, I would go for a drive. That day, I was so upset that I drove all the way to Baton Rouge, yelling, crying, and beating on the steering wheel, telling God how unfair it was that He was letting him get away with all of this. Finally, I wore myself out, turned around, and headed back to New Orleans.

That's when I heard the Lord say, "Now are you finished with your temper tantrum?" I said yes. Then He said, "You are going to go to court, but when you do, I want you to ask him to forgive you."

I couldn't believe what I was hearing.

"Evidently, you have forgotten about all of the things he has done!" I told God and then proceeded to remind him of my ex-husband's shortcomings.

Then God said, "Yes, that is true, but haven't you relished the thought of him burning in hell for all eternity?"

I began to weep.

"Yes, Lord, I have." I remembered that every time I would hear about something he had done, I would say to myself, "That's okay, he is going to burn in hell."

"I will ask him to forgive me, God, but you have to help me," I prayed.

Not long after that, I got a notice for a new court date. The day came, and I felt like I had hands wrapped around my throat. I wanted to ask for forgiveness but couldn't get the words out. When the court recessed for lunch, God said, "You will not see the judge until you ask for forgiveness." I asked Him to please help me.

When we came back from the lunch break, I walked up to my ex-husband, and the look on his face was shock and surprise. I literally choked out the words. I told him I knew he wouldn't understand what I was going to say, but I asked him to forgive me. I told him how I had relished the thought of him burning in hell. The moment I asked for forgiveness, it felt like a ton had been lifted off me. Before my ex-husband could say a word, the bailiff opened the door and called us into court.

There we were before the judge. This had been a long time coming. The judge threw the book at him and told him he wanted $1,500 in court by Wednesday, or my ex-husband would be spending Thanksgiving in jail. I hurried out of the courtroom, surprised to realize I felt bad about what had just happened.

This showed me that God was truly doing a work in my heart, as the anger I had felt toward him was gone. I got to my car and began to drive off when my ex-husband flagged me down and stopped me. I told him how sorry I was. He said that he would not have believed me if I had not apologized before we went into court. He then apologized to me and said he deserved the actions of the judge, who also ordered him to pay thirty-five dollars a week in child support. I did receive the $1,500, my ex-husband stayed out of jail, and the judgment for the support was to start the following week.

I learned something very important from this experience.

God showed me how forgiveness isn't for the
person who has hurt you; forgiveness is for you.

When you hold unforgiveness in your heart toward someone, it releases poisonous chemicals in your body without you even realizing it. Unforgiveness is the root cause of many diseases. It opens the door for the enemy to attack you physically. It also leaves your soul in a dire state as bitterness creeps in. It also stops any blessings God wants to give you. Your relationship with God is greatly hindered, and you can't grow spiritually or receive what He may have for you.

Forgiveness sets you free. It doesn't mean you have to stay in a relationship with the person who hurt you. It does, however, set you free from pain, turmoil, and strategies the enemy can use against you because of the doors that bitterness opens in your heart.

Looking back, I think forgiving my ex-husband released blessings on me and my daughter, both spiritual and economic. Tuition was fifty dollars per semester. I was able to get student loans for college and nursing school, which helped a lot. Jesus was right. I didn't have to worry about money. I could work at the hospital in the daytime and attend college at night.

I began taking all my prerequisites for nursing school, but I was constantly unsure of myself. When I think about what I would say to myself and all the time I spent dwelling on the negative, I shake my head. That garbage just wears you out, and you don't even realize it! I would have had much more energy if I had worried less.

> *"You will find true success when you find me, for I have*
> *insight into wise plans that are designed just for you. I hold in*
> *my hands living-understanding, courage, and strength."*
> *– Proverbs 8:14 (TPT)*

When I started nursing school, my schedule was tighter and tighter. I spent my weekends studying. Eventually, it was so demanding that I couldn't work. I was living off student loans and grants, and my mother and I were pooling our money just to make ends meet.

My brother had remarried and had his own business and his own house. He was making $4,000 to $5,000 a month, yet he would call my mother and ask her for money. When it was time for me to pay the rent, sometimes I was short. I would call him, and he always said, "I don't have it. What do you want me to do?" This only made our relationship worse.

Chapter
EIGHT

ONE NIGHT, not long after I started nursing school, my brother called. It was after midnight, and I had to be at the hospital at six in the morning. He asked me where my mother was.

"Asleep," I replied. "Where else would she be?"

He said he had to talk to her and that she couldn't go to work the next day. I asked why, and he said, "I got busted by the feds, and I have to turn myself in tomorrow." He told me he had been charged for making ecstasy in his chemical lab. I was furious. I woke my mother, gave her the phone, and went back to bed. The next day, he turned himself in to the police and went to jail. One of his friends bailed him out and helped him get an attorney.

He went to court and was found guilty, but before he was sentenced, the court sent out an investigator to talk to his family and friends. He called me to tell me this and then said, "I told the investigator about you and dad."

God had been working on me and was ever so gently starting to heal me. You could have punched me in the stomach when he told me this—another betrayal. I was thrown under the bus to make this investigator feel sorry for him and the family he had come from. He was hoping this information would lighten his sentence.

I told my mother what he had done, and she never said a word. Her silence spoke volumes to me and reinforced my feeling that he had always been her favorite. She would get into arguments with my dad, and I remember my dad telling her how she always made excuses for my brother and would justify everything he did. This time, she didn't even try to make an excuse for him. She just sat there in total silence.

After the investigator left, I told her that if she ever gave my brother any more money, I was finished with them both. She said not to talk that way, that we were family, and he needed us. I was sick and tired of always being expected to step up to the plate and help him. When were we ever going to have a normal life?

My brother was sentenced to eighteen months in federal prison at Eglin Air Force Base in Florida. His wife and son worked hard to keep the business going while he was away. He did his time and returned home.

By the time he returned, I had begun to feel like life was being sucked out of me. The tension and arguments with my mother were becoming volatile. Between her and my brother and living like we were, I was becoming suicidal. I had come to the point of planning how I would do it. My daughter was the only reason I held back.

Let me say this: I understand how a person can commit suicide. You get to a point where you feel there is no hope and that the situation you are in or the life you are leading will never get any better. You just want to stop the world and get off so you don't have to feel any more pain, live through any more crises, or experience any more drama. I just could not see how life would ever get any better. I felt trapped in a web of lies, control, and manipulation.

My mother was becoming even more controlling when it came to my daughter. I could see she was beginning to feel like my daughter was hers. It was becoming sick and more dysfunctional with each passing day. We were her life, as she would so often remind me. I finally told her she needed her own life, but she didn't understand what that was.

I began to see that her entire life had always been wrapped up in crisis and drama. That was the only way she knew how to function. Either she was living in the drama of my dad and his life choices, or my brother was creating chaos and tragedy. Both of them were addicted to crisis, living in flight-or-fight mode daily. Neither could understand why I was pulling away from them.

When I reached out to my brother for help with Mom, he would say, "I will talk to her," but he never did. Again, he was too wrapped up in his own life and couldn't see the spiritual ramifications that were taking place. He was busy settling in to being back home and starting his life over.

Life for me was becoming unbearable. I didn't know how much more I could take. My thoughts of suicide were getting stronger and stronger. At the time, I didn't know how my father's suicide contributed to my thoughts of suicide. I was in so many spiritual battles and growing very weary. At one point, I took a bottle of sleeping pills and woke up thirty-six hours later, disgusted that it didn't work.

In the summer of 1986, while in nursing school, I had a hysterectomy. I was off for the summer, so it was a good time to get it done. While recuperating, I was lying on the couch one day, reading a book entitled *The Pursuit of God* by A.W. Tozer. My daughter was outside playing with one of her friends.

While reading, a presence began to manifest over me. The only way I could describe this was a weighty, heavy, sweet presence like warm oil. It started at my feet, then would go up to my head and roll back down to my feet. Each time it returned to my feet, it became heavier and heavier. It got so heavy that I felt like I was being pressed through the couch and then down to the floor. I had to ask for it to stop, as I felt like my bones would be crushed if it didn't.

Gently, it began to lift. By this time, the book I was reading had fallen on my chest, and I picked it up to look at the cover. The cover had a picture of a deer in a field, and suddenly, I was in the field! I stretched my hand out and touched the deer's back. He turned and looked at me. I could feel the hair on his back, the sun beating on me, and the grass against my legs. I began to walk through the field. Then the thought hit me, "Where am I? How did I get here? And, oh my gosh, how do I get back? I have to go. What if my daughter needs me?"

Instantly, I was back on the couch. The sweet presence was still there with me, and I felt a "knowing" that I had just had a miraculous encounter with another dimension of heaven. Mary was the only person I told about this encounter. She said she wasn't surprised, as the Lord had told her I would experience a miracle, and this was definitely a miracle.

> *"I know a man in Christ who fourteen years ago was*
> *caught up to the third heaven—whether in the body*
> *or out of the body I do not know, God knows."*
> *– 2 Corinthians 12:2 (ESV)*

Life went on, and we continued to struggle. Soon it was time for my daughter to start school. In New Orleans, public school was rough. You didn't put your child there unless you had to.

My mother went to a Catholic Church, so we thought it best for my daughter to attend their school. There weren't many nuns, and I kept a close eye on things. My mother knew I wasn't raising my daughter to be Catholic, and this was causing a mild amount of friction in the house.

"Why are you sending her to a Catholic school if you are not going to raise her as a Catholic?" she wanted to know.

I reminded her that she was going there to get an education, not religion.

Things began to get tense. I was in school and still attending church, Bible study, and intercessory prayer meetings. My mother started telling me she wouldn't keep my daughter when I would go to Bible study. No problem; I just started taking her with me. My daughter started going with me to Bible study and intercessory prayer meetings on Friday nights too. Most of the time, we didn't get home from prayer meetings until one or two in the morning. We didn't have to get up early on Saturday mornings, so that was fine with me.

However, this didn't sit well with my mother. We would fight over how late I was coming home and how long we were in church on Sundays. She would say, "I'm in and out of church in thirty minutes. I don't see why you stay for hours."

I tried to explain to her that it wasn't about religion; it was about relationship and that we loved being at church. I told her she should be happy I was at prayer meetings instead of in a bar. My daughter was growing up with me in school, she was in school, and we were going to prayer meetings, picnics, parks, and whatever else I could find for us to do.

Looking back, taking my daughter with me to Bible study and prayer meetings was one of the best decisions I ever made. She grew up under an anointing that continues today.

> I encourage parents to keep their kids in the church
> and a prayer group. It does wonders for them.

One weekend, I took my daughter and nephew to Houston to Astroworld. I was looking forward to getting out of the city and spending time with my daughter without my mother being there. I prayed and asked the Lord to bless the trip and bring my daughter and me closer together.

While we were at Astroworld, I lost the car keys. I had no idea where they could be, as we had been there all day and it was then ten o'clock at night. I sat down with my daughter and told her we had to ask her dad where the keys were. I was raising her to know that God was her dad since my ex-husband was never a part of her life. We both prayed, and instantly, God showed me exactly where the keys were. My nephew sat with her, and I went to the first ride we had gone on. There they were in a basket full of other keys.

My daughter was beginning to see God answer so many prayers for us. Her faith was growing in leaps and bounds. She also walked in an unusual amount of favor wherever she went.

One morning, I was sitting outside reading my Bible when my daughter came out and crawled up on my lap.

"Mommy, if I tell you something, will you promise not to tell Grandma?"

I told her I promised and that she could tell me anything. She said my mother had been telling her not to listen to me about what I was teaching her about God.

I knew God was showing me how my mother was trying to undermine what I was doing. I put it in the back of my mind and never said a word about it.

Not long after our trip to Houston, my daughter came home with information from the church about making her first confession. The paper from the school said the priest takes the place of Jesus in the confessional. I knew I had to take a stand, and I knew it would cause another disagreement with my mother, and it did.

Our arguments intensified, and I could see how it started affecting my daughter. She was being pulled in two directions. She loved my mother, and she loved me. She was being put in the middle, and my mother was trying to get her to take sides.

My mother had dramatically changed since my father's death. When he was alive, she had no life of her own. Her world revolved around us and our home. Now, she was becoming angry and bitter all the time. She wanted to have the final say when it came to raising my daughter, and she wanted to be in control of everything.

My feckless brother had given her free rein with his kids, but I was not about to let that happen. God had blessed me and entrusted me with this incredible child. She was my responsibility and no one else's. I was committed to raising her in the admonition of the Lord. I knew how important my role was as her mother, and I was not about to give that up.

At the end of her first grade year, we went to the awards ceremony at my daughter's school. The principal, preparing to present an award, said, "This is the most prestigious award that St. Benilde gives to a student. It goes to the student who most exemplifies Christ." That award was given to my daughter.

The parents around me turned to me and said, "You're not Catholic! How can she get that award?" I told them I didn't know and that they should take it up with the principal. God truly has a sense of humor and does things to try and open our eyes to the truth. I knew this would be another argument when we got home, and it was.

Again, I tried to explain to my mother that it's not about religion—it's about relationship and knowing Jesus on a personal level. She could never understand it.

One night, I had another dream. In the dream, my daughter and I were dressed in our finest clothes and were seated at a banquet table with the finest china, silver, and candles. We were so excited. Men were dressed in white, wearing big chef hats. They were carrying large silver trays loaded with food.

I looked toward the end of the table when two men came up, carrying a big white sack. My eyes were fixed on the sack. One of them reached down and pulled out of the sack a slimy green overstuffed frog.

At that moment, I heard my daughter crying, and still dreaming, I got up to go and find her. As I started walking, I looked to my left, and it was pitch black. Out of that darkness came my mother. She said, "I know why she is crying because look what it did to me." She turned her face, and there was a hole in the side of her face with blood dripping down. Then she opened her hand, and there was a golden stinger with little hairs on it.

I woke up and jumped out of bed, knowing God was trying to tell me something. I asked God to give me three people who could tell me what the dream meant. That morning, I called Mary, told her about the dream, and asked if she knew what it meant. She said, "You and Amanda are in the kingdom and were at the banqueting table. The frog is a spirit of perversion. Your mother is demon-possessed with that spirit of perversion, which came from your father."

"The reason Amanda is crying," she said, "is because that demon knows it can't get you, but it's going to try and get to Amanda." Then she asked, "How can you live with someone who is demon-possessed?" I told her this was my mother and that I had a responsibility to take care of her.

The next confirmation came from an evangelist who came into town to preach at our church. I went to dinner with her after church and told her about the dream. She gave me the same interpretation.

The third confirmation came from a preacher who came to the church and testified about when he had a ruptured aneurysm and died. He said two angels came and took him and showed him how the kingdom of darkness is set up. He said that at one point, he was in a cafeteria-like setting and saw a man and a woman facing each other and talking. They were unaware of the frog-like spirit between them. This frog-like spirit kept jumping up toward the man's face and then finally jumped into the man's face, and the angel said, "possession complete."

The preacher then said, "This can occur with small children," but he couldn't remember the circumstances that would allow this to happen. Well, I had my three confirmations.

I struggled with all of this. I kept saying that she was my mother and I had to take care of her.

> When you are truly seeking the truth,
> God will give you scriptures to confirm it
> to you if you spend time with Him.

He gave me Matthew 10:35–36: "For I have come to set a man against his father, and a daughter against her mother, and a daughter-in-law against her mother-in-law. And a person's enemies will be those of his own household." *(ESV)*

Chapter
NINE

IT TOOK ME FIVE YEARS to complete school. It wasn't as difficult as I thought it would be. However, there were times when I didn't have a babysitter, so I would take my daughter to classes with me. My instructors never said a word because they knew that was the only way I could come to class that day. My daughter surprisingly enjoyed going to class with me. She would sit quietly at the desk next to me and listen intently to everything presented.

There were also times I would have to take her to the hospital with me when I had to do research in the library, and she would help me make copies of the materials I was researching. I would make deals with her, like promising to take her to eat in the cafeteria at the hospital or taking her to swim in the doctor's pool on the hospital roof. That was her favorite activity. These times with her were rewarding, and she could see what it took for me to get through school.

The night I was to graduate, she came home from school that day not feeling well. I remember telling her she couldn't be sick as I graduated that night and wanted her there. I will never forget her response. She looked at me intently and said, "Mommy, even if they had to carry me in there on a stretcher, I'm not going to miss this."

I realized then that she had a stake in my graduation and had worked alongside me to help me get there. This was as important to her as it was to me.

In my senior year of nursing school, we were at the VA hospital doing our final rotation. One morning, after getting my assignment, I went into my first patient's room to assess him. I noticed the side rails were up, and he was short of breath. I asked him what was wrong. He said he had to go to the bathroom and couldn't get anyone to come, so he climbed over the side rails to go to the bathroom and climbed back over them to get back in bed. In mid-sentence, he coded. I threw the side rails down, jumped into the bed, hit the code button, and began CPR. Everyone came running. He was stabilized and taken to the ICU.

After a while, the ICU nurse manager and nursing supervisor came looking for me. I instantly thought I had done something wrong and that my career was over before it had even started. Instead, they asked me to come and work for them in the ICU, which is unheard of. They offered a six-week intensive ICU course, a preceptor I would buddy with, and after a year, I would be on her rotation but work independently. She would still be available to help me if I needed it.

It was a dream come true, as that was my heart's desire. I so enjoyed my time at the VA. I loved working with the veterans. They were always so kind and appreciative of anything you did for them.

The fights between my mother and me only intensified after I finished nursing school. Our tiny apartment gave me no privacy or place to get away from her. Having my daughter in the middle of it was difficult as well.

Things got worse as we argued more about church and not raising my daughter as a Catholic. One night after one of our arguments, I went into my room and fell on my knees. I didn't pray—I couldn't even think of a prayer—but something came out of the center of my being and went straight up. Basically, it was my spirit crying out to God, telling Him that if He didn't do something, I would physically die here.

> *"Yahweh, don't condemn me. Don't punish me in your fiery anger. Please deal gently with me, Yahweh; show me mercy, for I'm sick and frail and weak. Heal me, Yahweh, for I'm falling apart. My soul is so troubled; but you, Yahweh—how long?"*
> *– Psalm 6:1–3 (TPT)*

The very next day, I opened my Bible, and it fell open to Ezekiel Chapter 12, which stated: "Son of man, you dwell in the midst of the rebellious house, who have eyes to see, and don't see, who have ears to hear, and don't hear, for they are a rebellious house. Therefore, you son of man, prepare you stuff for removing, and remove by day in their sight; And you shall remove from your place to another place in their sight: it may be they will consider, though they are a rebellious house." – Ezekiel 12:2–3 *(HNV)*

My mind began to race, and I thought, "They are going to want to know why I'm doing this."

A few paragraphs further, it said, "Son of man, has not the house of Israel, the rebellious house, said to you, 'What are you doing?' Say to them, 'Thus says the Lord God: This oracle concerns the prince in Jerusalem and all the house of Israel who are in it.' Say, 'I am a sign for you: as I have done, so shall it be done to them. They shall go into exile, into captivity.' – Ezekiel 12:9–11 *(ESV)*

Well, I thought, this would take another ten years, but then the last paragraph said:

"Therefore say to them, Thus says the Lord God: None of
my words will be delayed any longer, but the word that
I speak will be performed, declares the Lord God."
– Ezekiel 12:28 (ESV)

I was shocked. I said to the Lord, "If you are telling me to go, I will need at least $1,500 to move because I have no money." I called Mary and told her what the Lord had said.

Three days later, I got a call from the hospital where I worked. It was my day off, but I was asked to come in for a special meeting. I went in, and the head of the hospital entered the room with a stack of envelopes in his hand. He said there were eight ICU units in the hospital, and our unit was the only one where they were having problems keeping nurses. He said, "Today we are giving you a $1,500 bonus, and in three months, another $1,500, and then in six months, another $1,500 bonus to add up to a total of $5,000."

When they put that check in my hand, I cried. I knew it was God who was delivering me and setting me free. I called Mary, and she told me not to tell my family and to open a separate checking account, which I did. I began looking for a place close to Amanda's school and found a two-bedroom apartment. It had wooden floors and was beautiful, full of peace and light.

I rented the apartment on October 31. God told me to begin to take Amanda there on the weekends so she would get used to it. We would go to our new home and camp out for the weekend. Amanda knew not to say anything to anyone, as I told her we would move when God said it was time to go. She understood and said, "Let's see if we can make it on our own."

She knew how bad things had become between my mother and me, but she also knew she had to stay quiet to keep the peace. November came, and I told the Lord I couldn't move then because it was Thanksgiving, and they would say I ruined their Thanksgiving. December came, and I told God I couldn't move because it was Christmas, and they would say I ruined their Christmas.

January first came, and my mother and I were both sick with the flu. God spoke to me again and said, "Tell her. Now is the time. You won't get well until you tell her."

I was terrified. The phone rang. It was Mary.

"The Lord told me to call you and tell you He is sitting right next to you and that you are to tell her you are moving," she said, with no idea that I was sitting there trying to tell her. I simply said, "I know. I am trying."

Amanda went to take her bath, and while she was in the bathroom, I choked out the words, "I'm moving. I found an apartment, and we are moving."

World War III hit again. She began to yell and scream. She asked why I was doing this. I told her God told me to.

That's when she began to yell, "Your God told you to do this? What kind of a God do you serve?"

I went into the bathroom and told Amanda to get dressed because we were leaving. When I got in the car, I began to cry. My eight-year-old daughter put her little hands on my face and said, "Mommy, there is only one God, and evidently, she doesn't know Him."

Out of the mouths of babes: I was astonished. We went to the apartment, and I called Mary, and we prayed. Then, when I knew my mom would be in bed, we returned home.

That next week was very tense. By this time, my mother had notified everyone in the family about what I was planning to do. My brother was furious with me. I guess he was afraid he would have to let her live with him. I didn't care. I knew if I didn't get out of there, I would kill myself. I couldn't take it anymore. The life was being sucked out of me, and I was getting fragile.

In the meantime, my brother told my mother he would add on to his house so she could move in with him. She told me, "You can move when he finishes doing that." I told her, "No, we are moving at the end of the week."

"You have kept me from being conquered by my enemy; you broke
open the way to bring me to freedom, into a beautiful, broad place."
– Psalm 31:8 (TPT)

Everything happened just like the scripture said. My daughter and I carried everything out on our backs while my mother and family sat and watched us. No one would lift a finger to help us. I eventually got some friends to help me move the furniture.

We had our beds, bedroom furniture Mary had given us, and other incidentals we needed. The day we moved in, I told my daughter not to unpack everything because I felt we would not be there for long. At this point, we were just thrilled to be in that apartment. It was a place of refuge, but it also became a place of deliverance and healing.

As I became comfortable there, the Lord began to surface memories I had unconsciously buried. As these things started to resurface, I felt like I was having a breakdown. I could work twelve-hour shifts and perform my job, but when I was off, I could barely get out of bed. I would get my daughter off to school and then go back to bed. Conversations, memories, and traumas all began to surface—things I had buried from long ago. There were periods of my life that I couldn't remember; some years were just blank.

I remembered a conversation with my mother, telling me the family wanted her to take my brother to a psychiatrist when he was eight or nine. Of course, she said there was nothing wrong with him. As I began to think about this, it was revealed to me that my brother had played with me in an inappropriate way when I was very young. Then I began to understand why I had this love-hate relationship with him.

I remembered another conversation my mother had with me when I was about fourteen years old. She came to me and said rumors were going around accusing my father of having an inappropriate relationship with his business partner. I then understood why his partner wanted out of the business. At the time, my family didn't understand why this man had turned so viciously on my dad since they had known each other for years and had, at one time, been close friends. They didn't understand why he was so intent on destroying my dad.

This man was married and had twelve children at the time. My dad was charismatic and manipulated people into doing things they would never normally do. I began to see the depth of my dad's perversion and how this had been a curse passed down from generation to generation. Tears would stream down my face; all I could do was call on Jesus and ask Him to help me.

One night, after my daughter had gone to bed, the Lord spoke to me and said, "Open that chest." I had a wooden chest with all kinds of old family pictures in it. When I opened the chest, I felt a presence come out of it. I sat there for hours going through the photos and threw a lot of them away. This was a cleansing process.

That apartment became a place of safety and refuge for me as well as a place of great revelation and deliverance. I was like an onion whose very thin layers were being stripped away, one at a time. You never realize the bondage you are in until you experience some freedom and deliverance.

My mother began calling me and demanding to see my daughter every weekend. I told her this would not be possible since I had to have time with her. She insisted and then said, "This is like a divorce." I told her I was not married to her and that I had not had these types of orders or arguments with my husband when I divorced him, and that this was becoming sick and dysfunctional.

My daughter turned nine in February, and my mother called and asked to see her for her birthday. She wanted to throw a party for her. I told her that was fine, as I had to work. On her birthday, my mother took her while

I went to work. That night at about eight o'clock, she brought her home. My daughter came running in, crying, and when I asked her what was wrong, she said, "I'm so glad I'm home. All Grandma said all day long was, 'You knew about that apartment, didn't you? Why didn't you tell me?'"

I told my daughter it wasn't her fault and to go and take her bath, that I would deal with it. I then called my mother and told her she had better never put my daughter in the middle of us again, that she was only nine years old. She deserved to have as peaceful a life as I could give her, and that didn't include fights between us. My daughter had never seen my husband and me argue but was now being put in constant turmoil by her mother and grandmother fighting.

Then I said, "You knew what was happening to me when I was growing up."

Of course, she denied it but then said, "What was I supposed to do? I had never worked a day in my life. How was I supposed to take care of you and your brother?"

"So you sacrificed me for your comfort," I said.

"No, I didn't know," she replied.

"Yes, you did. You just admitted it."

I hung up the phone. The next day, I bought an answering machine. I didn't want to talk to any member of my family anymore. They had all been so critical and judgmental of me, especially after I decided to move away from my mother. They would say things like, "How could you leave her after all she has done for you?"

At the same time, they never acknowledged how I had put my mother through school and helped her get on her feet after my dad died. I was beginning to put up boundaries, limits that had never been allowed in my family before. Instead of my mother trying to mend our relationship, the demon in her would push her to places of more rage and control. Even though I was living in my own apartment now, the pressure and tensions from my family never abated.

"Let my passion for life be restored, tasting joy in every breakthrough you bring to me. Hold me close to you with a willing spirit that obeys whatever you say."
– Psalm 51:12 (TPT)

Chapter
TEN

MY DAUGHTER WAS IN THIRD GRADE and had started to struggle in school due to the stress we were having with my family. Spring break was coming up, so I thought it was an excellent time for a change of scenery. I decided to take her to Georgia so she could spend some time with my ex-mother-in-law.

The morning we left, it was pouring down rain, and as I drove across the causeway, my daughter fell asleep. I was listening to the radio, and the song "Shepherd Boy" came on. God began to minister to me through this song. The lyrics say that although others may see us as insignificant, like a shepherd boy, God may see us like David, as a king.

In an ordinary moment, in an ordinary life, He can touch you, and everything will change. I began to cry as God's presence filled that car, and with each passing mile that I drove, I could feel layers of pain flying off me. It again felt like the skin of an onion being peeled—light and very freeing.

God spoke to my heart and said, "I'm doing a new thing. I have a plan for your life. Everything is going to change."

"His light broke through the darkness and he led us out in freedom
from death's dark shadow and snapped every one of our chains."
– Psalm 107:14 (TPT)

I was on cloud nine and flew all the way to Georgia. Once we arrived, I was able to think clearly. Being away from the stress of my family and the heavy oppression I was under, I began to see things plainly. I thought about how I've always hated living in New Orleans. The city is under so much oppression due to voodoo and witchcraft's long history and practice there.

I thought, "I'm a nurse. I can get a job anywhere."

I decided to go to the VA hospital to see if they had any openings. I spoke to the head nurse in one of the ICUs. She had an open position and asked, "How would you like to work two twelve-hour shifts and get paid for forty hours?"

It was a Baylor position, something I had never heard of. I would work every weekend but be able to be home with my daughter during the week. I could be there for her when she came home from school every day.

She even said she would hold the position for me until my daughter got out of school in May. I jumped at the chance of being able to get out of the turmoil and control we had been under. Once again, God was moving on my behalf. He was making a way where there seemed to be no way.

My mother-in-law said she would babysit my daughter on the weekends when I worked. God was opening a door for me to finally be set free from all the oppression, control, and manipulation. This would give us some peace, and at the same time, it would be good for my daughter to get to know my ex-husband's side of the family.

CHAPTER TEN

When we headed back to Louisiana, I told my daughter that God was moving us to Georgia and that we would leave in May when she got out of school.

Since her dad was never really in her life, I had always raised my daughter to know that God was her father and that whatever He told us to do, we would do. We were going to follow Him and serve Him. Even to this day, she tells her friends, "God was in the house." She grew up with Him living with us, and we would talk to Him about everything.

"He was and is my daddy," my daughter says.

I taught her that she could crawl up in His lap and talk to Him about anything. I taught her to ask Him for whatever she wanted or needed. Many times, she would pray about something, and He would always answer her prayers. As we drove back to Louisiana, I explained to my daughter that we couldn't tell anyone we were moving because we would never be able to leave if we did.

The closer we got to the time for us to leave, the more nervous I was about my mother finding out we were moving. I felt like we were backed up like the Israelites against the Red Sea. The Lord told me to hide my car so my mother would think we weren't home if she drove by the apartment.

Finally, the day came for us to leave. I hired three men to load up the moving truck I had rented. God had a friend help us by driving the truck to Georgia, and I drove the car. The day we left, I stopped at my daughter's school to pick up her report card. Later, I would find out that we missed my mother at my daughter's school by ten minutes.

My daughter and I cried all the way to Mobile, Alabama. I told her I knew she didn't understand why we were leaving but that she had to trust that I had heard from God and that we would follow Him and do what He said. After we had been on the road for a while, it dawned on me that I had hired three men to load the truck but didn't have anyone on the other end to help me unload it. I began to cry out to God, asking Him for help.

I wondered if what I had done was really what God had told me to do. It's funny how the enemy will come to you and plant seeds of doubt in your mind. You begin to doubt yourself and doubt God. I just kept praying and begging God for His help.

When we got to Georgia, I took the truck from my friend and drove to the apartment we had rented. The parking lot was empty. It was the middle of the day on a Wednesday, and everyone was at work. My ex-husband's sister and her boyfriend came to help, but it was still going to be difficult to unload the furniture since there was only one guy among us.

When I opened the back of the truck, I looked at my daughter and said, "Come on, sweetie, we have to unload the truck." I remember her looking up at that mound of furniture as I handed her a small box and told her to carry it into the apartment. When we came back out, three men were standing by the side of the truck. They wore blue jeans, work boots, and no shirts. They asked us what we were doing.

"We're trying to unload this truck," I told them.

"Well, we will do it for you," they said.

My daughter and I looked at each other, and I said, "Okay." I asked them where they were from, and they said, "Around here." I asked them if they wanted something to drink, and they said no. I asked if they wanted something to eat, and they said no. I remember thinking how strange they were and how tan they were. They barely spoke to us.

After they finished, I went into the apartment to get some money out of my purse to pay them. When I walked out, the men were gone. I looked all around but couldn't find them. I kept asking, "Where are they?"

My daughter was pulling on my shirt, saying, "Mommy, Mommy!"

I finally said, "What?"

"Mommy, those were angels," she said.

"You knew?" I asked.

"Yes, I thought you knew," she said.

My knees almost buckled. God had miraculously come through for us again.

> Know this: whatever God calls you to do,
> He will provide and bring you through.

"Refuse to worry about tomorrow, but deal with each challenge that comes your way, one day at a time. Tomorrow will take care of itself."
– *Matthew 6:34 (TPT)*

This began a journey of many miracles. God stuck closer to us than a brother or a mother, and we could always feel His presence with us in the house. He is a Father to the fatherless and a husband to the husbandless. I began to see that He is all anyone ever needs. He will be just what you need Him to be.

My daughter began to experience God as her Father more profoundly than ever. It took time to settle in, and my daughter had the summer to adjust to our new life before starting school. She was also getting to know her grandmother and her cousins who lived there.

Within twenty-four hours of our arrival, my mother tracked us down and found where we were. She called my mother-in-law, but I told my mother-in-law that I didn't want to talk to her and didn't want my daughter to speak to her. At first, she respected my wishes, but after a while, she began to ask me to let my daughter have contact with my mother. She couldn't understand why I wouldn't allow her to talk to her.

I finally sat down one day and told her about my past, which was a big mistake. She knew me when I was in high school because I had spent some time with her when her son and I had been friends.

"Why didn't you tell me what you were going through?" she asked. "You could have come and lived with us."

I sensed she didn't believe me. In her mind, I had been this sweet, normal girl from a good family who never showed any appearance that anything was wrong. This was later confirmed when she told me she had asked my ex-husband if it were true. She said he told her it was. That surprised me, as I had never told him anything about that or my family life. Again, it made me feel like it was my fault for not telling her. I didn't even try to explain any more to her.

Our relationship was strained as it was because of the divorce, and I didn't want my daughter to lose another family member. I have to say, despite it all, she respected my wishes.

When my mother realized she wasn't getting anywhere with calling, she began to send money to my ex-sister-in-law's kids for Christmas and birthdays. She called them and was constantly trying to get information from them. It was quite humorous to me because when my mother-in-law lived in New Orleans, she would pass by our apartment every day coming home from work and never stopped to see my daughter or even call and ask about her. As a result, my mother would say things like, "What kind of woman doesn't want to see their own grandchild?" My mother didn't like her, but now they were close friends.

It was sickening to me, but my daughter began asking me to let her talk to my mother. I had to tell her we were not going to have any contact with her ever again. This subject became off-limits for us, like the proverbial elephant in the room that no one talks about.

I began to pray and ask God to explain this to my nine-year-old daughter because I didn't know how to. I prayed and prayed but had to wait on God. My daughter finally stopped asking, as she knew when I said no, it was no.

That fall, she settled into her new school and made many friends. The schools were different because they actually encouraged kids to dream big and be as creative as they wanted to be. My daughter wrote a book about our move to Georgia and then produced a video on being a newscaster. I was thrilled to see how she was beginning to blossom. Everyone at school seemed to like her, and she walked in great favor wherever she went and in whatever she did. I had told the teachers that the move had been hard on her, and they were kind to her and helped her in any way they could.

The following summer, I sent her to a Christian summer camp. It was an hour south of us, and she loved it. We were doing all kinds of fun things like camping, hiking, whitewater rafting, and, of course, shoe shopping, one of her favorite activities. I knew that deep down, she had the desire to go back to New Orleans, even though we never discussed it.

God remained faithful to us. When my daughter was twelve, she asked me to buy her a house. I was dumbfounded. What twelve-year-old wants a house? I told her we didn't need a house because when renting, we could move if we didn't like the way things were. I didn't understand at the time that she was tired of moving until she said, "That's the point. I don't want to move anymore."

I began to work even harder and told her I would try to get her a house. It was close to Christmas, and I had been working three jobs to save money. Finally, the loan came through, and I bought a house. That Christmas, my daughter got a house and a cat. We named the cat Noel since we had gotten her for Christmas, and on Christmas Eve, we put up our Christmas tree and slept in sleeping bags in front of the fireplace. We were thrilled. The day after Christmas, we moved in.

Our house had three bedrooms, two baths, and a twenty-by-twenty-foot sunken living room with a screened-in porch. It was an older house and needed a lot of cosmetic work, like painting, stripping wallpaper, flooring, and carpeting. God came through again. We lived there for six years, and within that time, that house was completely remodeled. People would come to visit and say things like, "This is a showplace." It was incredible what God did. It was so beautiful.

One time, the water heater leaked and flooded down the hallway into the kitchen and the living room. I paid the $250 deductible, and the insurance company replaced all of the flooring. We got new carpet and a new kitchen floor. This is just a small example of how God will turn around all things for your good. We loved that house and had so many good memories there.

> *"Yahweh, you alone are my inheritance. You are my prize, my pleasure, and my portion. You hold my destiny and its timing in your hands. Your pleasant path leads me to pleasant places. I'm overwhelmed by the privileges that come with following you! The way you counsel me makes me praise you more, for your whispers in the night give me wisdom, showing me what to do next. Because I set you, Yahweh, always close to me, my confidence will never be weakened, for I experience your wraparound presence every moment."*
> *– Psalm 16:5–8 (TPT)*

One night, God's presence woke me up at three in the morning. He was standing at the foot of my bed. I couldn't see Him, but His presence was undeniable. I said, "Yes, Lord, what is it?"

"It's time for you to forgive," He said.

I began to cry and told Him I didn't know how to forgive my family for the betrayal I had so deeply experienced.

"I have no idea how to do that," I said. "God, because You say I have to forgive, I will choose to forgive, but You will have to help me and show me."

It was a process, a very long process. I knew I was getting there because I was able to start praying for them and their salvation. That's when I knew I was on the right track. That's when I knew I had finally forgiven them.

As I said before, forgiveness isn't just for the person who wronged you. It is for you. I didn't even realize that I was carrying unforgiveness toward them because I was wrapped up in the daily routines of life. God, in His loving kindness and mercy, showed me. To this day, I thank Him for that.

Chapter
ELEVEN

I WAS SO HAPPY WITH WHAT GOD HAD DONE for us that I would go outside and pray over the house and walk around the yard, praising Him and thanking Him for what He had done.

During this time, we had a neighbor move into the house next door to us. He was Jewish and a single parent as well. One day, I noticed that my landmark was out of the ground, lying in the grass. I picked it up and put it back in. The next day when I went out to pray, it was lying on the ground again, so I put it back. The third day I went out, it was on the ground, but the next-door neighbor was in his yard this time. I asked him if he knew who kept taking my landmark out.

"I did," he said. "We don't need that. We are neighbors." I picked it up, shoved it back in the ground, and went into the house to call a friend. I asked if she would send her husband over to cement it in. He was kind enough to come and do it.

At the time, I didn't realize why this bothered me so much. I couldn't understand why a man would deliberately remove a property marker. I knew the Lord had given me this land and this house. I had marked it for Him, and I knew it was special. In essence, this man was crossing a boundary that was clearly defined.

Not long after that, my neighbor began to remodel his house. I came home one day, and he had put all his old flooring and carpet out in front of my house. I suppose that's why he didn't need a landmark between us. I would drag it back in front of his house only to discover it back in front of my house the next day. This went on for a few months. Again, it was as if he was crossing a boundary with no respect for my land.

He had been dating a lady and decided to remarry and rent out his house. His tenants were two men and a woman. They had seven boa constrictor snakes, many chow dogs—too numerous to count—three cats, three frogs, and a chameleon. They put up a fence for the dogs, but that didn't stop them from jumping the fence and trying to bite my daughter when she got off the school bus. They howled under my bedroom window all night long. I was working twelve-hour shifts in the ICU at the time and wasn't getting much sleep. Later, I discovered they had taken three feet of my property when they put the fence up.

I talked to these new neighbors and tried to reason with them, but they insisted it was another neighbor's dogs doing this. I would call animal control every time the dogs got out, and they would come and get them, but the neighbors would just go and pay the fine and bring them back. One time, I called the police at three o'clock in the morning. They said, "Lady, there's nothing we can do." I called my former neighbor and was told he wouldn't do anything because he told them they could have animals. I went to the county commissioner's office, and they refused to do anything.

One day, I came home because my daughter was sick, and the female neighbor was standing out in the driveway, waiting for me. She started yelling at me and said, "The next time you have a problem, you need to come and talk to us, not our landlord." I became incensed and told her this was not Africa and not a zoo.

"You need to take your fat ass and your menagerie of animals and move to the country," I said.

At that point, my daughter came out and pulled me into the house, worried about the neighbors hearing me. I told her I didn't care if they heard me, that I was sick and tired of not getting any sleep.

This went on for another week, and then one day, when my daughter came home, I told her to get in the car because we were going to find my former neighbor's new house. She said, "You don't know where he lives." I told her I knew the subdivision and that I would find him if I had to knock on every door. We drove to the subdivision and saw his kids riding their bikes. I asked where their house was, and they pointed it out to me.

"I'm not getting out," my daughter said as I pulled into the driveway.

"Fine," I said. "This will only take a minute."

My former neighbor let me in, and I again asked him if he would do anything to help me with the situation. He told me no. They were paying the rent, and that was all that mattered to him.

"Let me get this perfectly straight," I said. "You don't care what you have inflicted on me or the rest of the neighborhood as long as your pockets are lined with their money. Is that right?"

He basically said yes.

"Okay, that's all I need to know," I said.

I walked out, got in my car, and started to drive off when I slammed on the brakes and said, "Wait a minute, I've got to pray."

"Don't do it," my daughter said. "Don't do it."

"I'm doing it," I said.

"Don't do it, Mom," she pleaded.

"I'm doing it," I said.

Rolling the window down and stretching my hand toward his house, I began to pray. At the time, I didn't understand about the courtroom of heaven. However, it was the beginning of a greater revelation of God the Judge. I presented to the Lord everyone I had gone to about my problem, how I had appealed to the landlord, the renters, the police, and the county commissioner's office, and that He was the only one who could help me. I began to feel power coming out of my hand toward his house. I had never felt that before. I then asked for Him to empty the house, let it sit vacant, and then empty his pockets of all that money in the name of Jesus.

After that, I drove home and walked up and down my driveway, praying for God to drive them out. Every day, I would blow the shofar at the house and ask God to drive them out. Sometimes, I would be out on the driveway blowing the shofar when my daughter got off the bus.

"Mom, do you have to blow the shofar while I am getting off the bus?" she asked.

I told her I wasn't deliberately blowing it when she was coming off the bus and that I wasn't concerned with what people thought, as they weren't living in my shoes or paying my bills.

"We're not going to see these people in five years," I said. "Why should you care? This is a spiritual battle, and God is the only one who can deliver me from this situation."

This lasted about six weeks. Then one morning, I smelled something burning in my house. It smelled like an electrical fire. I asked my daughter if she could smell it, and she said no. I smelled it in the house twice. The next day, I was driving to work and smelled it in the car. I realized God was trying to tell me something, so I began to pray for protection over my house. We had had some work done on it, and I was worried.

That afternoon, my daughter called me at work.

"Mom, come home, the house next door is burning to the ground, and the fire is in the trees over the roof of our house."

I told her to get out of the house and call the fire department and that I was on my way home. When I got there, the fire was out, and our house didn't have any damage. The house next door had burned to the ground. Firefighters had hosed down my home and the trees.

I jumped out of the car and praised Jesus. I felt like Miriam, who had crossed the Red Sea. God had delivered me!

My daughter came out and dragged me into the house.

"Mom, you could at least act like you feel bad for them," she said.

"Why would I do that?" I said. "I am thrilled that God has delivered me. I didn't tell God to burn the house down. I just asked Him to drive them out. It was His choice on how He wanted to do it."

My only wish was for them to move out, which would allow me to sleep at night and have peace. I also wouldn't have to worry about my daughter getting bit by their dogs. We also had to watch our little dog because they could have easily attacked her. We both were fearful when we walked out of our home, and it was daunting, to say the least. At that moment, I realized more than ever that God was ever watchful over us and knew every detail of what we were going through.

"Mom, they are going to think you did it," my daughter said.

"Don't be ridiculous," I said. "I was at work all day."

The next thing I knew, the doorbell rang. I opened the door to someone from the fire department.

"Before I answer any questions, I just want to know, are the snakes gone?" I asked.

"The snakes are dead, and they are all gone," he said. "No one can come back to that house."

"Good," I said and invited him in.

He just wanted to reassure me that my house was okay but to contact the insurance company in case they wanted to come out to check it. I thanked him, and he left.

Later, I found three scriptures that pertain to removing your neighbor's landmark: Deuteronomy 27:17, Proverbs 22:28, and Proverbs 23:10–11. The last scripture is very specific about not removing the landmark or entering the field of the fatherless.

> *"Never move a long-standing boundary line or attempt*
> *to take land that belongs to the fatherless. For they have*
> *a mighty protector, a loving redeemer, who watches*
> *over them, and he will stand up for their cause."*
> *– Proverbs 23:10–11 (TPT)*

Christians have accused me of praying witchcraft prayers. However, how many times in the Bible do we read about God as Judge?

> *"When justice is served, the lovers of God cele-*
> *brate and rejoice, but the wicked begin to panic."*
> *– Proverbs 21:15 (TPT)*

> *"Jesus continued, 'Did you hear what the godless judge said—that*
> *he would answer her persistent request? Don't you know that God,*
> *the true judge, will grant justice to all his chosen ones who cry out to*
> *him night and day? He will pour out his Spirit upon them. He will*
> *not delay to answer you and give you what you ask for. God will*
> *give swift justice to those who don't give up. So be ever praying, ever*
> *expecting, in the same way as the widow. Even so, when the Son of*
> *Man comes back, will he find this kind of undying faith on earth?"*
> *– Luke 18:6–8 (TPT)*

Don't worry about what other people say or think about you. Your salvation and the way you live for the Lord are between you and the Lord.

I never claimed to be perfect. That is what is so amazing about the Lord. He works with you every step of the way if you continue to yield to Him and ask Him to be the Lord of your life. If there is something He doesn't like, He will let you know ever so gently. Then it is up to you whether you will make the necessary correction He is asking you to make.

> We all have a free will; He will never push Himself on us. Now, if there is a lesson He is trying to teach you, and you don't get it, you may have to repeat the lesson again and again until you finally realize what He is asking of you.

This was the beginning of me learning another aspect of who God was to me and how, no matter what would happen, I could always trust Him and know He was always there for me.

Chapter

TWELVE

WHEN MY DAUGHTER WAS A SOPHOMORE in high school, she was having trouble with math. I found a tutor for her, and she would stay after class to get help. When it came time for her final exam, she had to make a seventy-six to pass the course. The morning of the exam, I was driving her to school and started to pray for her. As I prayed, I told her, "You are going to do good on this test. No, you are going to do real good on this test."

"I hope so," she replied feebly.

She went to her class and sat in front of the teacher. The teacher knew how nervous Amanda was. As Amanda started to take the test, she began to cry.

"Just pray," the teacher, who was a Christian, said.

My daughter tried to do the first two problems and then prayed. As she started to work on the third problem, she began to hear in her spirit the letters a, c, and d. She thought, "Well, I might as well go with that since I don't know what I am doing."

She took the whole test, answering the questions with the answers she was hearing in her spirit. At the end of the day, she got her grade. It was a ninety-six. She missed the first two problems she tried to work on her own.

I was thrilled for her but did tell her that God was not always going to do that for her. The reason He came through was that she had done her very best and asked Him for His help. This was amazing to both of us, another miracle and lesson of trust.

I continued to send my daughter to the Christian camp she had been going to for years. I would drive her there on a Sunday evening and pick her up on a Friday evening. I had continued to pray that God would show her why we had to leave New Orleans in the past, as it was still a subject we did not discuss.

She became old enough to start working as a camp counselor. One week, she was at the camp, babysitting the pastor's kids all week and working in other areas, too. The pastor's wife came to her on Thursday morning and told her that the Lord had spoken to her and said Amanda should be in the service that night. She told my daughter that she would get someone else to babysit for her. My daughter was working in the kitchen that evening, so she was a little late getting to the service. When she walked in, the preacher was already preaching.

He stopped and said, "The Lord wants to take this service in another direction." He walked over to someone helping him with the worship music and told him to put on a particular song. It was "Shepherd Boy," the song my daughter had heard me playing when she was growing up.

Again, she heard how others might see you
as ordinary, but God may have plans for you
that no one imagines. In a moment, He can
touch you, and everything will change.

My daughter had a vision and was taken by His spirit back to New Orleans to the first apartment we lived in with my mother. She said she looked down into it and saw two little lights walking around. Then black tornadoes would start spinning, threatening to overtake us. The light would get very bright, and the tornadoes would bounce off us.

Then the Lord took her to that first apartment we moved to. They walked in, and it was very bright. The Lord told her, "You and your mom are in the light and of the light." Then He took her outside and told her to look over the city. It was totally black, and then bars started coming up all around her. The Lord told her, "If I hadn't taken you and your mother out of here, I would never be able to accomplish the plan and purpose I have for your lives."

"For you are all children of the light and children of the day. We don't belong to the night nor to darkness."
– 1 Thessalonians 5:5 (TPT)

It was two in the morning when she called me crying.

"I finally know why we left New Orleans, and the desire to go back has been completely taken away!" she said.

I had prayed for that moment for six solid years. I cried because of God's great faithfulness. He waited until He could show her in a way that she would understand. My daughter's relationship with the Lord was growing deeper and deeper. She was seeing Him move mightily in our lives and was learning how to rely on Him for her needs.

My daughter loved shoes. One day, she asked me to buy her a seventy-five-dollar pair of shoes. I told her I wasn't paying seventy-five dollars for shoes and that if she wanted those shoes, she would have to ask her dad (meaning God) for them. A few months later, after having that conversation with her, we were shopping and came across a shoe warehouse. We decided to check it out. Inside were rows and rows of shoes. I had never seen one store have so many shoes. She went to one side of the store, and I went to the other side, and we would meet somewhere in the middle.

As I started walking down the aisles of shoes, lo and behold, there were those seventy-five-dollar shoes she wanted. Only they were fifty dollars. The Lord spoke to my heart and said, "Buy those shoes." Of course, I began to argue with Him, saying that I didn't want to buy them even though they were fifty dollars.

He said, "I said, buy those shoes."

I called my daughter over, showed her the shoes, and told her that her dad told me I had to buy them. Well, she began jumping up and down, yelling, "My dad came through again!"

When I got to the register to pay for them, they took another 50 percent off, so they were only $25. Again, more repenting.

When would I ever learn not to argue with the Creator of the universe?

The following summer, it was time for Amanda to return to the summer camp to work. Mary had come into town and was leaving on Sunday morning at six to return to New Orleans. I woke up Amanda and told her to come into the living room to pray with us. Being a teenager, she really didn't want to get up, but I insisted. She went into the living room and sat on the sofa as we began to pray.

Suddenly, Mary began to say that a spirit of sudden destruction and calamity will try to come against Amanda.

"We come against you in the mighty name of Jesus," Mary prayed.

We began to war in the spirit. When we finished, I asked her what she thought it could be, and she said she didn't know. Mary left, and that evening, I drove Amanda down to the camp. I was to pick her up on Friday. That

Thursday, I was at work seeing patients when my pager began to go off with the camp number and a 911 page after the number. At first, I thought Amanda was calling to tell me to pick her up early, so I didn't answer it right away. I got two more pages and decided to call them. It was the camp asking if I was Amanda's mother.

"Yes, this is she," I said.

They began to tell me that Amanda was found unconscious at the bottom of the ten-foot pool. They thought they had gotten all the water out of her lungs, but she was on her way to the hospital by ambulance.

Amanda was a certified lifeguard and had completed the highest level of water safety. She could outswim and out dive the best of them. This was mind-boggling. How could this have happened?

I immediately left work and headed to Forsyth, Georgia. I began to storm heaven and beg God for her life. The peace of God filled my car, and I knew God was with me, but I didn't get an answer, just His peace. When I got to the hospital, she was awake and sitting up on the gurney. I asked what happened, and the nurse said she regained consciousness in the ambulance just before they got to the hospital. They gave her some oxygen in the emergency room, but there were no serious injuries, and she was released.

When we left the hospital, we stopped at a nearby restaurant. As I sat down, the reality of what had happened began to hit me, and I began to shake all over. Amanda then told me what had happened.

She had taken the pastor's kids to swim, and another counselor who wasn't supposed to be there happened by. Amanda had gotten out of the pool, wrapped her towel around her, and walked around the side of the pool to talk to the counselor. The counselor had climbed up into the lifeguard's chair with her back to Amanda. As my daughter was walking away, a metal prong from the skimmer basket popped up and made a puncture wound on the shin of her leg. She said the pain was excruciating, so she sat on the side of the pool and put her leg in the water to ease the agony.

The counselor continued talking to her but noticed she wasn't answering. The counselor turned around and saw a towel floating on top of the water and Amanda at the bottom of the pool. She had fainted and fallen into the water.

The counselor dove into the pool, pulled Amanda out, and began CPR. Amanda is five feet seven inches tall, and this girl was just five feet. I shudder to think what would have happened had we not prayed over her that Sunday morning. It showed me the power of prayer and how important it is to talk to the Lord.

One day, Amanda came to me and told me she had had a vision from the Lord. She said in the vision that we had opened our house for prayer. She saw cars lined up and down the street. She saw kids knocking on the door, thinking it was a party, then walking into the house and getting saved.

"Okay, let's do it," I said.

We started with about five kids on a Saturday night, and sure enough, it grew in no time. I had to move furniture out of the living room. Kids were praying, getting filled with the spirit, and then, just like she saw in her vision, kids came knocking on the door, thinking it was a party, and got saved.

It grew to about sixty kids coming on a Saturday night. It got so big I had to move it to the church. It didn't last long after we moved it there. The Lord told me to step down but to leave Amanda in it, as He would continue to use her. He told me it wouldn't be long before the pastor would shut it down. I told her about it, and she said she hoped it would last until the end of the school year.

Well, it only lasted for about another eight or nine weeks, and then the pastor shut it down. We were both disappointed. The kids didn't stay; they left the church. It was sad. Not long after that, we were shunned by the church. One member told me they were instructed not to speak to us. I didn't know what we had done to deserve that.

I was lying on my bed crying, and the Lord spoke to me in a stern voice.

"Get up. I'm going to talk to you," He said.

I went into the living room, and all I could find was my Matthew Henry's commentary, so I opened that. The page fell open to Jeremiah 12:5, which asks, "How can you run with the horsemen if the footmen weary you?"

Wow! I couldn't believe my eyes. I studied that chapter and four others for about five days with the Lord speaking to me. He really ministered to me through my study and comforted me in the process.

> Christians can hurt you. You just have
> to make up your mind that they aren't
> perfect, forgive them, and move on.

God is the only one who matters. Don't let anything or anyone come in between you and your walk with the Lord.

When it came time for Amanda to graduate from high school, I was standing at the kitchen sink washing dishes. I began to pray and ask God for money for Amanda's cap and gown, as I had already spent a thousand dollars on all the other senior things they needed. Her cap and gown were the last items she needed, and I didn't have the money.

Suddenly, Amanda came running into the house, screaming.

"Mom, I got a certificate in the mail for my cap and gown!"

The Lord spoke to my heart once again and said, "I'll answer you before you call Me." I looked at the certificate. It had come from a church we had never been to. It was from one of their Bible study groups.

God is so amazing. He is a BIG GOD who loves His children and takes good care of them.

The time for her graduation drew near, and we had been planning on using the Hope scholarship for her to go to college. One day, the Lord spoke to my heart and told me He did not want her to use that. He didn't want that money to touch her life. I asked Him what we were supposed to do.

"Trust me like you always have," He said.

I told my daughter, and she wanted to know what we were going to do, too.

"He is calling us to a deeper walk to increase our faith in Him and trust Him like we always have," I told her. We both agreed we would do what we felt like God was telling us to do. Many of our Christian friends thought we were crazy and had not heard from God.

Let this be a lesson to you.

> God calls people to all kinds of different things.
> If you feel God has told you something, then
> you follow God and not others. What's good for
> one may be totally different for someone else.
> He will frequently call you to walk a certain
> way and not require that of someone else.

Remember: this is a personal relationship you have, and He deals with His children the way we deal with ours. We don't treat all our children the same because they all have their own unique personalities. So it is with God's children as well.

Before Amanda graduated, God came through again. Mary had given her a piece of scripture jewelry she had gotten from a lady who imported it from Israel. Mary told us to go to the lady's house in case Amanda wanted to exchange it for something else. We went, and while we were there, the lady said to Amanda, "I feel like God wants me to ask you if you would like to sell this jewelry."

We asked what the cost would be, and she said, "Three hundred dollars to start." We told her we were very interested and would get back to her.

I was going to help my daughter, but God told me not to, that this was between the two of them. When we left there, we went to a friend's house to show her the jewelry, and she handed Amanda a card from another lady we had met only once. Amanda opened the card and found a seventy-five-dollar check in it for her graduation. When we got home that same afternoon, there was a check in the mail from the IRS to Amanda that she wasn't expecting. When we got in the house, there was a message on the answering machine asking her to babysit for an entire weekend. By the end of the day, she had more than $300 to start her business.

This all occurred in May when she was graduating. She called her enterprise Words of Wisdom. Little did we know that God would use that business to pay for much of her college expenses.

Chapter

THIRTEEN

IN THE FALL OF 1999, I heard from the Lord about two things. First, He told me to put the house on the market because He was moving us again. So, I put the house on the market and got a contract within a week. That was a shock, as I didn't know where we were going.

A nurse friend who lived out of town told me that another nurse friend was trying to contact me. She had opened an assisted living facility in the North Georgia Mountains and wanted me to come and work with her. I prayed about it and felt like this was where the Lord was leading me. So, we sold the house and moved to the North Georgia Mountains.

He also told me that He wanted Amanda to take a semester off before starting college. She began to worry, as she had always heard that if you don't go straight out of high school, you end up not going. Despite my objections, Amanda and one of her girlfriends planned to go to a community college. We argued about this. Finally, I told her that I was putting her in her dad's hands, as I was tired of arguing about it, and that I would ask Him to deal with her.

I was at work when I got a phone call from my daughter. I could tell by her voice that something was terribly wrong. She began to relate to me what had happened. She and her friend had gone to the college to register. They were there all day. The school had lost their transcripts, and as a result, they were told they would have to take all remedial classes.

They never found her friend's transcripts, but they did find Amanda's. They were outside of the financial office in her friend's car when Amanda said, "Wait, I forgot to pay." Her friend slammed on the brakes and said, "Hurry up!" Amanda got out of the car and walked around it to go inside to pay. As she did, her friend's foot slipped off the brake and onto the accelerator. The car hit Amanda, knocking her to the ground and rolling over her foot.

Her friend had driven her home. I enlisted another nurse to cover for me and went straight home. When I got there, I hugged her friend and asked if she was okay, then went over to the recliner where my daughter was. I looked at her foot and said, "Gee, that looks really painful."

"Yes," she said.

"Do you think that's where God wants you to go?"

"No," she said.

"Good choice," I said, "because I'd hate to see what He would do to you next time you are out of His will." Then I said, "Let's see how much mercy He will have."

I called the podiatrist who had previously performed surgery on her ingrown toenails. The receptionist said he wasn't in. I told her what had happened and asked if she would have him call in some pain medicine and that we would be there in the morning for surgery. Not even two minutes after I hung up, she called me back to tell me that the doctor had immediately called in pain medicine for Amanda.

I looked at her and said, "That's mercy."

This was a big lesson for my daughter. She learned what can happen when you are out of God's will. As a single parent all my daughter's life, I never had any problems with my child. She had always been a sweet, obedient child with a lot of wisdom for her age and walked in great favor wherever she went. This had been totally out of character for her.

Looking back years later, more was going on than what was in the eye's view. I took Amanda to college visits at every possible vacation opportunity, even when she was in kindergarten. I wanted to instill in her at a young age that college was the next step after high school. And as I stated before, Amanda attended schools that had raised her to think that if you don't go to college immediately, you will not go.

Both these situations allowed fear to envelop Amanda when it came to her abiding in the perfect plan God had for her, which was sitting out a semester. Now I see it wasn't rebellion, even though, at the time, it appeared to be. It was fear. As I have matured more in my relationship with the Lord, I recognize that it wasn't God who caused her to be hit by the car. However, it was His mercy to use this situation for her to see that favor wasn't on the community college plan and His protection was lifted.

It's important to consider how the plans we have for our children can shape their mindset. Even though I was doing everything I could to set her up for success, I now realize that this contributed to the fear she had when trying to decide what school to attend and God's timing on her beginning college.

The next day, my daughter had surgery to remove her toenail. It was quite painful, as the dressings had to be changed twice a day, and sometimes they would stick to the wound. It took a while to heal.

In the meantime, I told her friend she would have to help us pack to work off the surgery bill. The funny thing is that her friend's dad had asked what had happened to Amanda's foot. They told him one of Amanda's friends had run over her with their car. Her friend's father gave Amanda his attorney's card and told her to tell me to sue them.

"You need a new car, and he could probably get you $50,000 for pain, suffering, and surgery," he said.

We all laughed, and her friend told her father, "Dad, it's her friend. She's not suing her friend."

Years later, they told him the truth about what had happened. It was so funny for all of us.

"I should have known," he said.

In January, my daughter started college at a school not far away. I admit I was having a difficult time letting her go. After all, it had only been the two of us for all those years. I ended up leaving the assisted living facility, got a job in a hospital working in the operating room, and found an apartment twelve miles from where my daughter was in school.

At that time, I fell into a deep depression. God was still working on me, yet I was having a hard time with being alone. I was working in the OR, living in a tiny town, and seeing my daughter every now and then. One weekend, she came home and found me in my bed in total darkness, with the curtains shut and only the TV on.

She stood at the foot of my bed and cried. "I hate seeing you like this," she said. I told her to go back to school and that I had to feel this way until I didn't feel this way anymore. She left, and it took a while, but eventually, I came out of it.

Amanda was so happy at school. She walked in tremendous favor, and doors began to open for her. She was a resident assistant, which paid for her room and board.

While she was in that leadership position, God used it to teach her more of His ways in dealing with His people. In situations that would arise with other students, He showed her He loved mercy more than justice. She also learned it was lonely at the top. It's not a popular place to be when hard decisions must be made. Yet, in that place, He was grooming her for far greater purposes.

I injured my back working eighteen hours in the operating room. After being out of work for two months as a result, I knew it was time for me to find another place to work. I had herniated two disks and was praying for a job I could do that wouldn't strain my back.

One morning while praying, I had a vision of a large building. In the center of the building, I saw a flag flying from the rooftop. Later that week, I had a job interview with another hospital to return to the OR. I knew I couldn't do it, but I was desperate. I thought six weeks of orientation might give me more time to heal, and afterward, I could manage it.

While driving home after my interview, I saw a sign on the side of the road for a state prison. I had never noticed it before. Out of curiosity, I turned down the road to drive by it. The road took me through the backside of the prison, where I saw guards with shotguns standing in the watchtowers overlooking the facility. I realized they could see me driving, and it made me nervous. I also thought it wasn't what I saw when I was praying, so I was off the hook.

As I got to the stop sign and prepared to turn, that still small voice spoke and said, "Turn right." When I turned and looked to my right, I was in front of the prison. To my amazement, it was exactly what I had seen when I had prayed for a job. There was the flag flying in the center of the building. In utter shock, I almost drove into the ditch.

I pulled into the parking lot directly across the street and sat there.

"Lord, you can't be serious," I said. I can't do this or even consider this. I quickly left and drove home, telling myself they wouldn't have a job for a nurse. But when God wants you to do something, He will weigh in on you, and no matter what excuses you come up with, He will show you what He wants.

I called the prison and was told that, yes, they had nursing positions open.

"Would it be possible for you to come in for an interview on Tuesday?" they asked.

"Uh, no," I stuttered.

"Well, how about Wednesday?"

"No," I said.

"How about Friday?"

"Yes, Friday will be fine."

I needed a few days to get myself together before I could even consider walking in there. When Friday came, I was terrified. And when those gates slammed shut and locked, a wave of emotions hit me.

What was I thinking? Here I was, locked in with some of the most hardened criminals in Georgia.

I was taken on a tour of the medical building and given a description of the job responsibilities, salary, and benefits. I met the medical director and two other nurses who worked there. They asked how soon I could start once my credentials were certified.

"I have to think about it," I responded.

When I got home, I told the Lord, "You want me to take a $6,000 pay cut to wake up at the crack of dawn (4:00 a.m.) to go and work with a bunch of demons and devils? *No, I'm not doing it.* I can't! Don't ask me to do this!"

For three nights, I couldn't sleep. On the third one, I sat straight up in bed and said, "All right, I'll do it, but only out of obedience because You already know I don't want to."

It was the spring of that year when I became the triage nurse for one of the maximum-security prisons in the state of Georgia. It turned out to be one of the most rewarding jobs ever, quickly becoming my favorite job of my entire career. I absolutely loved working with the men and the doctor. Every day was a challenge, and there was never a dull moment.

The job entailed seeing the men who came to sick call. I would assess them and determine what level of care they needed. I enjoyed working with them and made it a practice not to ask what they had done to be there or how long their sentence was. I didn't want that information to taint the way I looked at them.

One day, I had a nineteen-year-old come to sick call, telling me he wasn't feeling well. I told him to get up on the table, and I began to assess him. I finally told him I couldn't find anything wrong and asked him to be more specific about his symptoms.

With his head lowered, he said, "I hear you talk to people."

I told him to sit down.

"When did you come into the system?" I asked.

"When I was fifteen."

Before I could say anything, he continued, "And I hope I spend the rest of my life here."

"Why?" I asked him.

"I murdered my sister," he said.

What came out of my mouth next was unexpected.

"Because she was sexually molesting you," I said matter of factly.

That's when the dam broke, and he began to sob and wail like I had never heard before. In between the sobs, he told me his mother was a single parent who had three kids. His sister was seven years older than him, and his brother was nine years old at the time.

His sister had been trying to pit his mother against him so she could get him thrown out of the house. He realized she wanted to begin abusing their younger brother, who was the same age he had been when she started to molest him. One morning after his mother had gone to work, he and his sister got into a fight in the kitchen. He told her he knew what she was trying to do and wouldn't allow that to happen to his brother.

In a rage, he pulled out a steak knife and stabbed her in the chest. I asked him if he had told his attorney or his mother what had happened.

He shook his head. "No. I didn't want to destroy my sister's memory."

He continued, "The day I was sentenced, my family disowned me and said they never wanted to see me again. My mother said, 'I have no son.'"

He told me the shame and guilt were more than he could take. He couldn't forgive himself for what he had done. He felt like his life was worthless, and he wanted to stay in prison for the rest of his life, but he would be up for parole when he turned thirty-eight.

I began to talk to him about Jesus and told him Jesus would forgive him if he asked. He just sat there sobbing.

After trying to console him and tell him he needed to forgive himself, I was able to hook him up with the prison ministry and a Bible study group. I also referred him to psychiatry.

"If you ever need to talk, just fill out a sick call slip, and I will see you," I told him.

This is just one of many stories I was told by different inmates. So many of them felt hopeless and lived with shame and guilt. There were so many lives there that had been destroyed by poor choices and rageful impulses. I knew Jesus was their only hope. I saw the Lord touch many lives while I was there, bringing hope to the hopeless.

On the other hand, some were hardened criminals and would cut your throat if they had a chance to. Those are the ones I could never figure out. What had happened to them to make them so cold and calloused?

What's funny to me is how I was allowed to talk to them about Jesus, but when working in the hospital, the administration discouraged us from sharing anything about the Lord.

After a year, the Lord told me it was time to quit.

"No way!" I told Him. "You called me in here kicking and screaming, and now it is my favorite nursing job ever. I am not quitting."

"Okay," He told me. "Then my hand of protection will not be on you."

"I'll put in my resignation tomorrow."

Four months later, I went to work at a psychiatric hospital to help troubled teens. I guess they figured if I could handle murderers, robbers, and rapists, I could handle troubled teens.

After Amanda graduated from the two-year college, she transferred to the University of Georgia in Athens, ninety miles away. This required more adjusting, as it wasn't twelve miles down the road where I could drop by. God is so merciful and knew how hard it was for me to let go, but I knew I had to.

This was an exciting year for her as she was getting an apartment with another girl—no more dorm room. I could see how happy she was, and it blessed me to see how she was growing. At first, she wanted to go to law school, but then she told me she decided on special education. This upset me. I told her special education professionals didn't make any money and that I couldn't support her for the rest of her life.

God got hold of me and told me to keep quiet. This wasn't about me; it was between them, and I needed to keep my mouth shut. More humble pie as I sat back and watched her graduate from the University of Georgia College of Education.

After graduation, she landed a teaching position in Peachtree City, Georgia. She had many offers, but this one stood out as they were just starting a new program for autistic children. They told her she could write her own program. This intrigued her, as she loves a good challenge.

On the other hand, I had more adjusting to do since Peachtree City was an hour and a half away. I had more time to practice letting go.

I was happy for her as she embarked on a new life and career. I was excited to see what God was going to do through her. God had shown me many times over the years that there was a special call on her life.

One of my prayers for her was that God would reveal to her at an early age His plan for her life. When she was about sixteen, she had a vision while in prayer one day. She said she saw a small school with a waiting list to get in. The kids would come in autistic and walk out completely healed and whole. Once again, God came through for her.

In the beginning, she had rented an apartment with another teacher. They were both just starting out, and teachers don't make much money. Sharing expenses helped. One day, one of her kids' parents told Amanda that a neighbor was selling a condo and asked if she would be interested in it. My daughter called me, and I encouraged her to go and check it out.

"We don't have any money for a condo," she began to tell me.

"Just go see it," I told her.

So she did. Afterward, she called and told me how nice it was and wanted to know if I would drive down to look at it with her. I drove down that night, and after seeing it, we went to the owner's house. There we were in the library of a multimillion-dollar home, discussing the purchase of this condo. We really didn't have any money to make that kind of purchase, but I knew from the past that God was a big God, and nothing is impossible for Him. To make a long story short, we got the condo for $1,500 down, and the owner paid the closing costs.

When I got to the car that night, I cried.

"What just happened was a total miracle," I said. "Your Dad came through for you again."

I explained that you usually pay 10 to 20 percent down plus the closing costs, which can run up to $5,000 or more. It was another miracle and provision from God, who was always taking care of us.

CHAPTER THIRTEEN

She got the condo but couldn't move in as she was still in a lease on her apartment. A close friend of hers needed a place to stay and lived there in the meantime, covering the monthly payment until her lease was up.

Amanda moved into the condo in May and began to settle into her career and life. I was living up in the mountains and working at a local hospital at the time. Life was good.

Chapter

FOURTEEN

ONE WEEKEND, I went to a Christian conference in the mountains near to where I lived. While I was in the worship service, I began to pray for my mother, but the Lord stopped me and said, "Don't pray for her."

When the service was over, I got in my car to drive home. It was dark while I drove through the mountains. I began to pray and told God I was confused about Him saying not to pray for her. Then I heard an almost audible voice in the car. It was a voice of judgment, and it scared me to death. I was bewildered, as I thought that since I had forgiven her, I was to continue to pray for her. I had never experienced the Lord's voice in that manner ever before.

"I am going to give her what she wants," the Lord said. "I'm going to give her your dad."

I began to cry and said, "Why? My dad is burning in hell. Why would you do that?"

"Because your dad is her God," He said.

That was a light bulb moment. That statement was so true, and it answered so many questions I had over the years. Memories of how my mother had been with my father and things I had heard her say flooded my mind. I began to cry.

When I arrived home, Amanda was waiting for me. I walked in crying, and she asked what was wrong.

"Your grandmother is dying," I said. As soon as those words came out of my mouth, it felt like claws were tearing at my chest.

Then I knew.

"Of lung cancer," I said.

We spent that whole weekend crying over her, mourning. At some point, I realized we were burying her in the spirit.

About six months later, my ex-husband called my daughter, asking for my phone number. She was very protective of me and told him she wasn't giving it to him. She asked what he wanted, and he told her my mother had called him and that she had lung cancer. She had undergone fifty-six radiation treatments, and they told her there was nothing else they could do.

She told him she wanted to see Amanda before she died and didn't care if she saw me. My daughter told him she would let me know.

When she called and told me what was happening, I told her I wouldn't tell her what to do. She was twenty-one years old, and I had raised her in the admonition of the Lord. I asked her to do one thing. I asked her to go and crawl up in her Dad's lap and ask Him what He wanted her to do.

"Whatever He tells you, I will abide by," I said.

She agreed to pray.

I began to storm heaven for her. I also called every intercessor I knew to pray for her and pray that she would hear clearly from God. About three days later, she called and told me she had heard from the Lord. I asked her what He said. She said she wasn't going.

The Lord told her, "The demon that lives in your grandmother will try to take you."

"You heard right," I told her and was relieved. I knew she had to hear it for herself. After God showed her what He had delivered us from when we were in New Orleans, it all began to make sense to her.

My mother didn't die for another seven years. Then, my ex-husband called my daughter again and asked for my phone number. Again, she told him she wasn't going to give it to him and asked what it was about. He said my brother had called and told him my mother had died. My brother wanted to cremate our mother but couldn't because I had to sign some papers to agree with his decision. She told him she would let me know.

Amanda called me and then told me the most shocking news. My mother had died on my daughter's birthday. Stunned doesn't begin to describe what I felt. The first thing I experienced was a tearing sensation in my spirit. Then I began to get angry at God. It was the first time in my whole life that I was angry at God.

"You had 364 other days of the year you could have taken her," I told Him.

My daughter's birthday was one of the happiest days of my entire life! How dare He ruin it for me!

I told Amanda to tell them to fax the papers to me, and I would sign and fax them back. I was getting ready for work when all this occurred, so I could stop at the bank and get the paperwork notarized and faxed back.

The next day when I was spending time with the Lord, I opened my Bible to a chapter in Ezekiel that talks about going down into the pit. I couldn't believe my eyes as I began to read it. In the spirit, I began to see my mother descending into the pit. There was a big pit, and there was fire and bubbling like you see in a volcano. There were caves all around it, and there were people in the pit and some in the caves. I saw my dad and other family members there as well. He was calling her and telling her to come. It broke my heart, and I wondered why God had let me see this. I still, to this day, don't know why I saw that.

After a while, I reasoned with God and told Him I didn't agree with what He had done but that I knew He does all things well and must have had a good reason for choosing to take her that day. Years later, I would find out why.

In 2010, we were blessed with buddy passes from one of the airlines. It was Christmas time, and we were trying to go to Israel. For two days, we tried to get out, but all the seats were full.

We decided to go someplace else, as we had already wasted two of the days we had off. At the airport ticket counter, trying to figure out where we could go, I asked the ticket agent, "How about Rome? I've always wanted to go there."

"Yes, there are available seats," the ticket agent said.

"Then Rome, here we come!"

It was a fantastic trip, and we saw the Vatican, St. Peter's Basilica, the Colosseum, and the Catacombs of Rome. In the catacombs, I got my answer as to why God had taken my mother on my daughter's birthday.

Out of nowhere, our tour guide, who was from India, said this:

"There's an ancient saying that when someone dies on someone's birthday, the person who dies goes to the place God has for them, and the person whose birthday it is, is then catapulted into the destiny God has for them. The soul tie is broken, and they are free to fulfill the plans and purposes God has for them."

I was shocked! I got my answer and again had to ask God to forgive me for not trusting Him, doubting His ways, and being angry with Him.

CHAPTER FOURTEEN

This was another incredible lesson of discovering who God is and how His ways are perfect and so much higher than ours.

PART THREE

The Flowers of the Lord

Chapter
FIFTEEN

AMANDA HAD BEEN WORKING in the public school system for three years. She loved working with the children, but I could tell she was beginning to burn out. I began to pray and ask God not only to help her but to give her some relief. I had no idea how He would do that.

At the end of the third summer break, she noticed a huge improvement in one of her students when he returned to school. He was surpassing all the goals that had been set for him. She asked his mother if she had changed his medication. His mom told her she had enrolled him in a program over the summer that worked on his brain.

Amanda got information about the program from her and decided to go and check it out for herself. Three doctors were running a program that worked with children with ADD, ADHD, dyslexia, and behavioral issues. It was a relatively new program and fell under the field of functional neurology.

Amanda attended a few of the lectures they hosted and began to ask many questions about how it worked. It intrigued her, as she was witnessing children truly being helped and changed. She saw how this program was getting to the root of what was causing the symptoms she was seeing. This was no Band-Aid approach, but true healing was occurring. As a result, these doctors offered her a part-time job making the same amount of money she was making as a full-time teacher. She jumped at the chance to be a part of something on the cutting edge of a technology that was truly getting results.

One day, Amanda came to me and told me to get my passport. Katrina had hit New Orleans, and she said I should get it now as it may take a long time due to the flood. Little did I know she was planning a big surprise for me.

In the meantime, I had a dream that I was walking on some old cobblestones. In this dream, as I looked to the left, there was a wall of ancient stones with flowers growing out of them. I woke myself up saying, "I never want to leave here. I never want to leave here."

One month later, Amanda announced we were going to Israel! I couldn't believe it! This had been a lifelong dream, and I never expected to see it fulfilled.

Then, three days before we were to leave, we both got bonuses from our jobs! The hospital where I worked had not given a bonus to its employees in nineteen years, yet out of the blue, here came this bonus. I knew it was the Lord giving both of us extra money for the trip. When we got to the airport and went to board the plane, they upgraded us to first class! We both got on the plane in shock. We kept saying, "Is this really happening?" We felt like princesses. Flying to Israel first class was the most incredible experience I had ever had.

A friend went to Israel with us and showed us around, along with the missionaries there. The next day, we were in the old city, and I asked if the

Eastern Gate was nearby. I told her I didn't care if I saw anything else but wanted to see the Eastern Gate. She said it was around the corner from where we were.

As we turned the corner, I was in the dream I had had, walking on the old cobblestones. As I looked to the left, there was a wall of ancient stones with flowers growing out of it.

I stopped, and my daughter and friend kept walking. God's presence fell on me, and I heard the Lord say, "When you first got saved and saw a picture of My gates, you said to Me, 'I want to go there. I want to see them; I want to touch them.' Today, daughter, you will touch my gates."

When my daughter and friend came to see why I had stopped, I was weeping. When I explained, our friend said, "Let's go!"

We tried to enter the gate, but Israeli soldiers with guns were guarding it. Our friend said she knew another way and took us to the Arab side. It was open with no one there. That day, I reached the top and touched the Eastern Gate, where I picked up some rocks and carried them back with me.

I had forgotten about telling the Lord I wanted to see the gates until He reminded me that day. He is so amazing.

> He never forgets one thing when it concerns one of
> His children. He is so into the details of your life.

He loves His children so much; all He wants is for us to come to Him, trust Him, and love Him. That day, I learned how much He listens to every word we utter to Him.

This had been a lifelong dream, and I had never thought it would come true. Yet, here I was in Israel, touching the very Gates I had only seen in pictures. God is so incredibly amazing!

That was only the beginning of what He had in store for us on that trip. We were there for a ladies' conference and were scheduled to leave earlier than the others. I kept telling my daughter I wanted to stay and I wasn't ready to go home. During the trip, I kept picking up rocks and putting dirt in bottles. I had never done anything like that before. My daughter kept telling me my suitcase would be over the weight limit if I didn't stop.

One morning, she was on the computer in the hotel, handling emails.

"Mom, my friends are all saying we are stuck here," she told me. "They are asking each other if I know that we are stuck here in Israel."

"They must be playing a trick on you," I said. I told her we should ask John, our missionary friend touring with us.

"Ah yes, my sister, I am afraid it's true," John said. "The airport has been shut down."

"For how long?" I asked.

"I don't know. It could be a few days, a week, or a month."

"We can't stay here for a month!" my daughter exclaimed. Then she looked at me and said, "This is all your fault. You have been telling God you didn't want to leave."

It was true. I did keep telling God I wasn't ready to go, as I wanted to stay longer. Suddenly, peace came over me.

"God has something for us to do here, and when we do it, then we will get out," I told her, "even if they have to send a plane to get us. "

This was so good, as we were able to finish the tour with everyone else. A South African woman on tour with us told John that the Lord told her to plant a tree in Israel when she was there. There were one hundred ladies on this tour, and I had told John not to worry about getting a tree for this lady, as he had too much to do with everything else he was handling.

We visited Gethsemane. While there, I looked down and saw a tree with the root exposed, lying in front of my feet. I picked it up and brought it to Amanda, John's wife. She took it to the lady, who became so excited that she started jumping up and down. They decided they would plant the tree at our next stop.

I kept taking pictures of the Eastern Gate.

"Don't you have enough pictures of the Gate?" my daughter kept asking.

"No," I told her. "I just have to take a few more."

The next place we went to was Caiaphas's house. The lady decided to plant the tree there. When they were finished, another lady got a word from the Lord.

She said, "God said, 'Two nations stand before me this day, an American who found the tree and a South African who planted the tree. I will hold these two nations in remembrance, and I'm calling my bride out of the church, and my bride will walk through my gates."

My daughter and I began to weep. The presence and power of God were so strong. No one could deny that He was there.

I then looked at my daughter and told her, "Now we will get out." We had stayed an extra three days, and I was thrilled!

The flights were all backed up because of the shutdown, so they did send an extra plane to fly people out. We departed that night on the eleven o'clock flight and, again, flew first class!

When we got home, I received a newsletter from Sid Roth. I couldn't believe what I was reading! He paraphrased Psalm 102:14: *my servants take pleasure in her stones and delight in her dust.*

I had my answer as to why I kept picking up the rocks and dirt to bring home. Since then, we have been able to return to Israel several times, and whenever I go, someone asks me to bring a rock back for them.

Around 2009, I went online to look for a Christian conference I could go to. I found one in Knoxville, Tennessee, by a church called Abiding Glory. It looked like fun, and I had that weekend off, so I called a friend to see if she would go with me. It was a three-day conference, so we booked it. This turned out to be one of the best conferences I have ever been to. The encounters I had with the Lord were incredible!

While in worship, which was amazing, this woman walked up to me and said, "You're a daisy," and walked away.

"They've got some real flakes coming to these things," I remember saying to the Lord.

His response was, "Really? Well, you're drinking wine that's not here."

Ouch! He was right because at one point, I began to taste wine. It was the most delicious wine I had ever tasted! It was sweet, and the more I tasted it, the more I wanted. I kept saying, "More, Lord, more," to the point that I was literally drunk! My girlfriend was experiencing the same thing. There we were, drunk as skunks, and it wasn't even noon yet.

Then I thought, well, maybe there is something to this daisy thing. So I said, "Lord, if you are trying to tell me something about a daisy, let me see daisies when I walk out of here."

When the service ended, we broke for lunch. When they opened the doors to the banquet room, we saw daisies as the centerpieces on the tables. I stopped dead in my tracks. This was too good to be true.

I didn't eat much or have much of a conversation with anyone because I was trying to figure out what God was trying to tell me about daisies. After lunch, we went back into the afternoon service. Again, His presence was undeniable. The worship was phenomenal, and I was taken into heaven by the spirit. I was walking next to Jesus, and flowers were everywhere.

As we walked, the Lord began to speak to me.

"All of my worshippers are like these flowers," He said. "When they worship, each one gives off their own fragrance, and my Father breathes it in, and they give honor and glory to Him."

"Why would you make me a daisy?" I asked him. "Daisies aren't pretty.

They don't even smell good. Why couldn't you have made me a rose or another kind of flower? What does a daisy mean?"

Suddenly, we were outside the throne room, and He had His hand behind His back. When He brought His hand from around His back, it held a huge bouquet of flowers, and I noticed a small daisy hanging on the edge of the bouquet. He pushed His hand into the throne room and said, "These are the ones I died for."

With that, I found myself on the sanctuary floor crying: "I'll be a daisy if you want me to!"

My girlfriend and I stayed drunk in the spirit for the entire three days we were there. Thank goodness we stayed in the same hotel the conference was in because we couldn't drive anywhere. Every night, we would fall into the elevator drunk and barely make it to our room. We lay in our beds, and the glory and presence of God would wash over us in waves.

The day came when we had to drive back from Knoxville to Georgia. We were still drunk, and it was in the afternoon before we could get ourselves together to even think of driving back. I was supposed to work that night but knew I couldn't. I kept telling the Lord I couldn't function. He had to do something.

A few hours before I was to report to work, the hospital called me and asked if I wanted the night off. I was so relieved that I didn't have to go in. It was the most exhilarating time I had ever spent with the Lord and one I will never forget.

Not long after this conference, my sixtieth birthday was coming up. Since we moved to Georgia, the Lord has always given me a birthday present. I told my daughter I was expecting something really big from Him because this was a big birthday. He has given me all kinds of birthday presents, but I couldn't imagine what this one would be. One day, she called me and said, "Mom, God has your birthday all figured out."

I got excited.

"What is it?" I asked.

She wouldn't tell me, just that, "You'll see."

A week before my birthday, my daughter called again and said, "I want to drive up and take you to dinner for your birthday."

I was thrilled, as she was taking me to one of our favorite places, Glen-Ella Springs, which is in the mountains of northern Georgia. When I got there, she had arranged for friends of mine from all over Georgia, Louisiana, and Tennessee to come for a birthday bash. I was so surprised and felt so loved to think everyone had come so far to celebrate with me. One person was missing, and that was Mary. She had died three weeks before my birthday. I was sad to think we couldn't celebrate with her.

As we all went into the restaurant, I saw sixty roses and a large gift bag on the table. My daughter handed it to me and said, "This is your present from the Lord." When I opened it, there was a vase, and on the rim of the vase were three heads. On the top of the heads were flowers. One was a rose, another was a purple flower, and there on the third head was a daisy.

The daisy's head on the rim of the vase was slightly tilted, with lips on the face puckered as if blowing something. I asked where she had found this, and she said she had gone to the home of a friend whose mom was a potter. She saw the vase and asked her what her inspiration was for that particular piece. She told my daughter that her mother had encountered the Lord in New Orleans, Louisiana, in 1977. He told her to pull over because He wanted her to write something. It was a poem entitled "The Flowers of My Heart."

She also gave me the poem to read, and to my astonishment, it was word for word what the Lord had told me at that conference. The only difference was in the poem, He said, "Wouldn't it be sad if the daisy wanted to be a rose? A daisy brings hope for tomorrow." I had my answer as to what a daisy meant.

My daughter noticed the face and said, "I never noticed that before. If I had, I would have picked another vase."

She had no idea what was coming next. Mary's daughter came to the party and presented me with Mary's shofar. Mary and I would sometimes go out at night and go where we were led by the spirit and blow the shofar. The face of the daisy head's lips was pursed like she was blowing.

The Lord is so incredible and loves each one of us intricately. He cares about every detail of our lives, down to knowing exactly how many hairs we have on our heads. He cares about decorating—yes, even that. He has always helped me pick out paint colors, furniture, beds, and whatever I would talk to Him about. He would always be interested and would give me His ideas and opinions.

People don't realize that the Lord who created everything is detailed, meticulous, and interested in all of His creations. He wants to be a part of our lives, even the mundane, everyday lives we may have. Not just the problems but the fun stuff too. It's not complicated to have a relationship with Him. I talk to Him like He's my best friend because He is.

Chapter
SIXTEEN

IN THE MEANTIME, I was getting older, and my body wasn't as young as it used to be. I was tired of the long shifts and didn't know how much longer I could keep up the grueling pace I had been working. One day, Amanda called and said, "Mom, I think you should retire."

At first, I said no.

A few months later, she called again.

"It's time for you to retire so you can get on with your life and do what God has for you to do," she said. "You can move into my condo, and I'll take care of everything."

Was I hearing her right? Who on earth would turn down a deal like that?

I retired and moved into her condo. The day after I moved in, I woke up, got some coffee, looked at my dog, and said, "Now, what do we do?"

I was worried I wouldn't like being retired and told myself I could always return to work if I wanted to. Well, I'm here to tell you that life took off for me.

I began traveling with friends and then got the idea to write this book. I started writing it, and after a while, I asked the Lord, "Is this worth finishing?"

A few days later, I went to an organic coffee shop with a friend. A lady I had never met came walking out of the coffee shop. She extended her hand and started to introduce herself. Suddenly, she put her hand on my stomach and said, "There's a book inside of you, and God wants you to write it because it will minister to a lot of people."

I was surprised at the way God chose to answer my question. That encounter encouraged me to continue to write. It took eight years, and then I told the Lord that I had no idea how to get a book published or what the cost would be.

Years earlier, when my daughter was working in Peachtree City, she met a woman who owned a local magazine. The publication featured articles about women and people who had businesses in the area, and they featured my daughter on the cover one month. By the time I finished the book, my daughter was living in Florida and working in her own centers.

On a trip to visit me in Peachtree City, my daughter encountered this woman again. She mentioned to her that I had written a book and was trying to figure out how to get it published. This precious lady offered to look at my book and give us her opinion on what to do. I dropped off the manuscript, and in just a few hours, she called and said she would love to work with me to edit the book and get it done. How exciting! God was opening a door and answering my prayer on how to accomplish this task.

When the editing was finished, I wondered how I would get the money together to pay for it to be published. My daughter had told me she wanted to cover the cost, but at that time, we had no idea what that would be. We scheduled a Zoom meeting with the editor to discuss the next steps and how to proceed. During this meeting, she gave us the cost to design and produce the book.

My daughter saw the look on my face and said, "Mom, exactly one hour ago, I got a call from a media company I work with, and they informed me I would be getting a distribution check." The amount was double what it would cost to get the book published.

God came through again! I almost cried when I heard this. He *never* stops amazing me. Just when I think I've seen all He can do, He shocks me back to the reality of realizing we will never be able to figure Him out. His ways are far beyond our ways.

Writing a book allowed me to reflect on my life and recognize the many amazing things the Lord has done for me. He used Mary in my life in so many ways. God used her to teach me about Him, pray for me, counsel me, and most of all, encourage me to become the person God created me to be. I will forever be grateful to her.

The trajectory of my life changed over a ten-year period because of that encounter. I became a nurse, moved out of the projects of New Orleans, moved to another state, and was truly happy for the first time.

I am blessed to have had such an exciting, rewarding career. I was able to work in so many fields of nursing, and with each new job, I learned something. In the end, it was all worth it.

The thoughts of not being able to do it and that I was not smart enough all faded over the years with the feelings of accomplishment, self-assurance, and self-worth. The fear of inadequacy that had plagued me years ago no longer whispered in my ear. Gone were the voices that echoed "You can't" or "You aren't smart enough." The many obstacles in front of me had disappeared, and victory was sweet. I truly can do all things through Christ, who strengthens me.

In my nursing career, certain cases stand out in my mind, forever etched in my memory. One such case happened in an intensive care unit at one of the hospitals where I worked to pick up extra shifts.

The patient I was assigned that day was a thirty-three-year-old blind woman who was in kidney failure. She had been diagnosed with diabetes as a juvenile, and the disease had caused her to go blind. She had also been addicted to various drugs throughout her life.

I was one of the many nurses who cared for her while she was in the ICU. Many of us witnessed to her about Jesus. I asked her if she knew Jesus, and she would always say yes.

On the day she died, she sat straight up in the bed with her eyes wide open and a look of horror on her face. She cried out, "The fire! The fire! The fire!" then fell back into her bed and died. To say this shook me to the core of my being is an understatement. I watched someone die in agony, horror, and great fear. There was no peace in that room that day.

On difficult days like this, I would sometimes go home in tears. I never reached a place of complacency when seeing someone die or suffer. I promised myself that if I ever felt that way, I would leave the profession.

I learned that when people are sick or in pain, showing compassion makes it a little easier for them, and they appreciate anything you do for them. I loved my patients and their families and never wanted to go into administration because of that.

There were many gratifying days of nursing when I would go home feeling like I had made a difference in someone's life. One such case I will never forget. While working in home health, I was assigned to see a male patient who had been in the hospital with flesh-eating bacteria. The bacteria had set up in his scrotum and required surgery. He was lucky to have survived this ordeal.

When he was discharged home, he required nursing visits twice a day to cleanse and pack his scrotum with sterile gauze, as they had to leave it open to allow it to heal from the inside out. On my first visit, this man was upset. He told me the doctor had ruined him.

As I began to take care of him, I reassured him that his manhood was fully intact and that he would be as good as new once it healed.

"Are you telling me the truth?" he asked.

"I've seen worse," I said. "You have nothing to worry about."

There was one problem, however. He liked to wear blue jeans.

"No more blue jeans until you are completely healed," I told him, and I had his wife go and buy him loose-fitting jogging pants.

This was a bone of contention between us, as he felt he could wear his jeans without any problem. One day, I had an unexpected assignment with another patient and had to pass him to another nurse for his morning visit. That afternoon, the nurse called me and told me she had seen him in his blue jeans on the corner of Main Street, talking to a blonde woman. I thanked her and then went to see him later that afternoon.

When I got there, he began to tell me how much he was hurting and how painful it was.

"Do you think wearing your blue jeans while visiting with the blonde woman on Main Street had anything to do with the pain you are experiencing?"

Shocked, he asked, "Do you have spies watching me?"

"Yes, I do," I replied. "And I better not find out you are in those blue jeans again!"

It took a few months, but he finally healed and was so grateful for all I had done to help him.

Although I've included many stories of the miraculous power of God at work in my life, many more come to mind. For instance, I took a nursing job at one of the local hospitals in Georgia. I was working in what they call the float pool, which meant they would send me to any floor or ICU unit that was short-staffed that day. I loved that position because I was able to work all over the hospital and meet more of my colleagues.

Every day was different, and I liked having a variety of cases. When I took the job, the Lord told me never to change the assignment I received; each assignment was for a purpose. There was only one place I didn't like to go, and that was the treatment room. It was really an emergency room. One day, I was told to go there.

"Darn," I whispered.

Another nurse overheard me and offered to exchange assignments. Just as I was going to take her up on her offer, I remembered what the Lord had told me. I thanked her but said I would go where I was assigned.

I wasn't in the treatment room long when a man came in having a heart attack. As I began drawing blood and hooking him up to the monitors, he began to talk about a place called the R Ranch. He was quite expressive, and I kept trying to quiet him down and told him to just rest. He insisted on talking about it.

"It relaxes me," he said.

As I was caring for him, he told me how he had bought a cabin for a dollar. He said three tornadoes had hit there, and people were selling their shares for a dollar. I told him if he ever found another one for that price to please let me know. He said he would, and then I transferred him to his room.

A few months later, the hospital called me, telling me a man had been calling them asking for my number. They, of course, wouldn't give it to him, so I took his number and called him. Lo and behold, it was the man I had taken care of in the treatment room. He was able to find another cabin for a dollar. I bought it, and that opened the door to a tremendous blessing for my daughter and me. Nestled in the North Georgia Mountains, this incredible place had canoes, horses, a game room, and waterfalls nearby. Our cabin had two bedrooms, a small kitchen, and a front porch.

I would arrange my schedule at the hospital so we could spend more time there. When I worked three twelve-hour shifts, I could have seven days off in a row before returning to work. I did that all summer long so that every other week, I would get off work, drive to our apartment, load up the car, then head to the mountains. We met all kinds of interesting people and had so much fun, and my daughter just loved it.

Had I changed my assignment that day, we would have missed out on one of the most incredible blessings God had for us. It taught me that obedience is better than sacrifice and that God has His very best for us. He has our best interests at heart.

We kept the cabin for three years and thoroughly enjoyed it. Eventually, I sold it, and my dollar investment turned into $1,500!

After being in the condo for a year, I got a call from Amanda, whose career had taken her from Atlanta to Kansas City. She told me the doctors in Atlanta called and offered her an opportunity to return and work with them. I was thrilled, as that would mean she was coming home. After much discussion, she decided to make the move.

I went to Kansas City and spent the summer there, helping her pack up and leave. After the movers left, we both drove our cars back to Atlanta. As she started working there, a well-known football coach called her. She had worked with his son, and he was pleased with the progress his son had made. He asked her if she would go down to Orlando, Florida, and see if she liked it and would like to open up a center there.

She had received offers like this before, but it just never felt right. She would pray about them but never got a green light. I told her she had to go and check it out. If she didn't, she would always wonder if she had made the right decision. This was a wonderful opportunity for her, a chance to own her own business, and who knows? Maybe more than one business.

She made a trip down to Orlando and stayed for a few days. When she came home, she told me how much she loved it and that the oak trees reminded her of New Orleans. Of course, now she was in a real dilemma, as she had already started working for the doctors in Atlanta. We prayed a lot before she made the decision to move to Orlando. When she told the doctors in Atlanta about her offer, they were supportive and said they understood and wished her well.

We took a few days and drove down to look for a house to rent. After looking at a few places, we walked into a house, looked at each other, and knew this was the one. It reminded us of our home in Lilburn so many years ago, except it was better. It had three bedrooms, two bathrooms, a large living room, dining room, kitchen, and an enclosed saltwater swimming pool that was incredible!

God spoke to me during the process of packing again and said that this house would be a home base for me, as I would be coming and going. I was overjoyed, as I love to travel and visit different places. After we moved in, I was amazed at how much traveling I began to do while she was busy opening her first business. Yes, I said her first, as she ended up owning three businesses.

We are both amazed as we look back and see how the hand of God took us from living in the projects of New Orleans to owning three businesses. The word astounding doesn't describe what God can do! God had told me that through Amanda He would redeem everything stolen from us, and He has. He is faithful to His promises and His word.

Chapter
SEVENTEEN

TO THIS VERY DAY, I often wonder why God came into my life and why, at the very point of my hopelessness and despair, He came and helped me. I certainly didn't deserve His attention. I had never given Him a second thought. To be honest, He was the furthest thing from my mind, and I certainly didn't think He could help me.

I still feel so undeserving of what He has done for me and how He has changed me. If I spent the rest of eternity saying thank you, it wouldn't be enough.

Even after all my experiences, I was and still am a work in progress. It's like the layers of an onion, peeled off one at a time. Those layers consist of shame, abuse, rejection, unworthiness, insecurity, anger, hopelessness, and any other thing the enemy can think of to put on you and make you believe that is who you are. Those layers cloud the person who Christ says you are. Those layers keep you stuck in a place of unbelief for anything good.

Jesus begins to show you who you really are and who He says you are. Your identity begins to change, and you become the person He says you are. You will never be perfect. You will make mistakes along the way, but you know you are not alone. He is walking with you every step of the way. The beauty is that you are forever loved and cherished. You can hide in the shelter of His arms, knowing that no matter what happens, He will make all things work together for your good. He even uses the muck, the mire, and the mud pits you walk in to change you for the better.

His love is so deep, so everlasting, and so good that no matter what you do, He loves you. He loves you just because He loves you. There isn't anything you could do that would ever change that. He loves you in spite of yourself.

Even when you fall, He is there to encourage you, forgive you, pick you back up, and help you move forward. The more time you spend in His presence, the more you want to be with Him. Everything else pales in comparison to Him.

He loves you too much to let you stay the way you are.

When you go through the trials of life, the residue left in you can lead to dark, gaping wounds that are raw and ever-present. They affect your body, soul, and spirit and can paralyze the person you were created to be. Everything you do, say, and react to is filtered through those wounds. The enemy uses all of that to keep you from the plans and purposes that God has for you.

How can you get set free? How can you change your life and escape the prison you are being kept in? I'm here to tell you it's coming to know Jesus Christ, trusting Him, developing a relationship with Him, and asking Him to come into your life and change you. It's putting your complete faith and trust in Him. It's a long process but so very worth it.

CHAPTER SEVENTEEN

There are two types of people in this world: those who empower their excuses and stay stuck in them and those who empower their goals and move forward. The difference between the two is perseverance. That is the key: to persevere. Persevere, no matter what. Persevere in every situation. He will give you the strength, courage, and fortitude to do just that. Along the way, your priorities will change, and you will realize that your ultimate goal will be to walk the path of life to the best of your ability so that you can be with Him for eternity. When that joyous moment comes, you will meet Him face to face and know it was so worth it.

If you have come to the place of wanting to give up, I encourage you to open your heart, tell Jesus you are at the end of your rope, and ask Him to forgive you of all your sins and be the Lord of your life. Tell Him you need Him and that He is the only one who can help you. Then watch what He does.

Your journey begins, and it will be the ride of a lifetime.

As you learn to depend on Him and include Him in your everyday life, you will experience wonders and miracles you never dreamed possible.

Over the years, I've learned to enjoy each moment, live in the now, and delight in whatever season I am in. I can remember a time when I couldn't even hear the birds sing. That was when life had been so hard and all I could think about was surviving. But God changed my life, and He will change yours, too. If you are sincere and open your heart to Him, He will do it.

Faithful and true, a father to the fatherless, a husband to the husbandless, a mother, a father, and a friend He will be. He truly does give you hope for tomorrow.

"You brought me back from the brink of death, from the depths below. Now here I am, alive and well, fully restored!"
– Psalm 30:3 (TPT)

Lord, I am amazed at how You have been so entrenched in my life. In the turmoil, brokenness, and pain, You came and carried me to places I never dreamed possible. I just don't understand why You would even look in my direction.

In the pain and desperation, I couldn't even see light or hope for anything better. I'm sad to say I didn't even give You a thought in the midst of it all. However, You came and literally breathed life back into me. You carried me, healed my wounds, and delivered me from total darkness.

Now, after all these years of living and walking with You and being on the other side of it all, I'm so very grateful that I stuck it out. Why? Because it has given me a chance to see that life can be good. That there are bright sides to it and that it is worth living. It also showed me I am stronger than I thought and that with You, ALL things are possible.

ACKNOWLEDGMENTS

TO JOYCE, the words "thank you" aren't enough. Your kindness, encouragement, and perseverance in helping me with this project are beyond anything I could have ever imagined. The hours you spent unselfishly working, perfecting, and advising can never be repaid. You will definitely hear those words we all long to hear one day, "Well done, my good and faithful servant."

To my friends who encouraged me in this work, thank you for the courage you gave me to write and share my story for His glory. Your support during this process has been inspirational. Thank you!

ABOUT THE AUTHOR

CATHERINE ALBEANESE knows what it means to be at the end of your rope. Her story is about how the miraculous power of God guided, healed, and delivered her from hopelessness and how He can do the same for you.

Catherine is an adventurer who loves fishing, camping, and hiking. As a child in the '50s, she was an avid scuba diver, spending many hours exploring Spanish galleon wrecks throughout the Caribbean with her family.

Now a mom, retired nurse, gardener, and dog lover, Catherine lives in the metro Atlanta area, where she enjoys spending time with friends, traveling with her daughter, and going to the dog park with her energetic Teddy Bear Shichon, Lady Liberty (Libby).

Contact Catherine at
fairhavenspublishing@gmail.com

Made in the USA
Columbia, SC
21 October 2024